THE SMITH'S WORK AND CLASSIC BLACKSMITHING TOOLS

CLASSIC APPROACHES AND EQUIPMENT FOR THE FORGE

BY **PAUL N. HASLUCK**

ORIGINALLY PUBLISHED IN 1904

LEGACY EDITION

HASLUCK'S TRADITIONAL SKILLS LIBRARY

BOOK 5

Doublebit Press
Eugene, OR

INTRODUCTION
To The Doublebit Press Legacy Edition

The old experts of artisanal trades, country and homestead knowledge, and the woods and mountains taught timeless principles and skills for centuries. Through their timeless books, the old experts offered rich descriptions of how the world works and encouraged learning through personal experiences *by doing*. Over the last 125 years, manufacturing, farming, and construction have substantially changed. Of course, many things have gotten simpler as equipment and technology have improved. In addition, some activities of pre-digital times are now no longer in vogue, or are even outright considered inappropriate or illegal. However, despite many of the positive changes in manufacturing and crafting methods that have occurred over the years, *there are many other skills and much knowledge that have been forgotten.*

By publishing *The Hasluck Traditional Skills Library*, it is our goal at Doublebit Press to do what we can to preserve and share the works from forgotten teachers that form the cornerstone of the history of the American artisans and traditional crafts. Through remastered reprint editions of timeless classics, perhaps we can regain some of this lost knowledge for future generations.

This book is an important contribution traditional handcraft and country skills literature and has important historical and collector value toward preserving the American handcraft and outdoors tradition. The knowledge it holds is an invaluable reference for practicing skills and hand craft methods. Its chapters thoroughly discuss some of the essential building blocks of knowledge that are fundamental but may have been forgotten as equipment gets fancier and technology gets smarter. In short, this book was chosen for Legacy Edition printing because much of the basic skills and knowledge it contains has been forgotten or put to the wayside in trade for more modern conveniences and methods.

With technology playing a major role in everyday life, sometimes we need to take a step back in time to find those basic building blocks used for gaining mastery – the things that we have luckily not completely lost and has been recorded in books over the last two centuries. These skills aren't forgotten, they've just been shelved. *It's time to unshelve them once again and reclaim the lost knowledge of self-sufficiency.*

Based on this commitment to preserving our outdoors and handcraft artisanal heritage, we have taken great pride in publishing this book as a complete original work. We hope it is worthy of both study and collection by outdoors folk in the modern era of outdoors and traditional skills life.

Unlike many other photocopy reproductions of classic books that are common on the market, this Legacy Edition does not simply place poor photography of old texts on our pages and use error-prone optical scanning or computer-generated text. We want our work to speak for itself, and reflect the quality demanded by our customers who spend their hard-earned money. With this in mind, each Legacy Edition book that has been chosen for publication is carefully remastered from original print books, *with the Doublebit Legacy Edition printed and laid out in the exact way that it was presented at its original publication.* We provide a beautiful, memorable experience that is as true to the original text as best as possible, but with the aid of modern technology to make as beautiful a reading experience as possible for books that can be over a century old.

Because of its age and because it is presented in its original form, the book may contain misspellings, inking errors from print plates, and other printing blemishes that were common for the age. However, these are exactly the things that we feel give the book its character, which we preserved in this Legacy Edition. During digitization, we ensured that each illustration in the text was clean and sharp with the least amount of loss from being copied and digitized as possible. Full-page plate illustrations are presented as they were found, often including the extra blank page that was often behind a plate. For the covers, we use the original cover design to give the book its original feel. We are sure you'll appreciate the fine touches and attention to detail that your Legacy Edition has to offer.

For traditional handcrafters and classic artisanal enthusiasts who demand the best from their equipment, this Doublebit Press Legacy Edition reprint was made with you in mind. Both important and minor details have equally both been accounted for by our publishing staff, down to the cover, font, layout, and images. It is the goal of Doublebit Legacy Edition series to be worthy of collection in any outdoorsperson's library and that can be passed to future generations.

Every book selected to be in this series offers unique views and instruction on important skills, advice, tips, tidbits, anecdotes, stories, and experiences that will enrichen the repertoire of any person who enjoys escaping a bit from today's modern technology-based, cookie-cutter, and highly industrialized skills. Instead, folks seeking to make things with their hands like the old days may find great value from these resurrected instructional manuals from the past. These books were not simply written to be shelved in a library – they contain our history and forgotten methods to make things with real character and energy with a *human* component.

Therefore, to learn the most basic building blocks of a craft leads to mastery of all its aspects. We hope this book helps you along this path with its rich descriptions and illustrations!

About Hasluck's Traditional Skills Library

Paul N. Hasluck was a prominent author on artisan skills and traditional handcrafts toward the end of the 19th Century. He was the editor of the magazine *Work*, which was a popular handcraft, shop skills, and artisanal craft magazine of the day. His broad expertise in making things with your hands led him to write or edit over 30 volumes on specific handcrafts, arts, and mechanics, with each manual containing invaluable information related to each craft.

Hasluck had a great eye for collecting the info that beginners and experts alike needed to perfect their craft. His volumes were loaded with helpful diagrams, tables, and illustrations that are useful even by today's digital standards. In short, Hasluck's instructional manuals were the *go-to instructional library* if someone wanted to learn a particular skill. Used by the U.S. military, the Boy and Girl Scouts, and countless folks at farms, public libraries, and homes across the world, Hasluck's instructional manuals were the perfect "handy book" for learning.

This Doublebit Press Legacy Edition republishes this tradition of handcrafted quality and artisanal work. We hope that this deluxe printed edition of this work will help you gain mastery in your craft, as it is presented in the exact form that it was originally published. Even today, the knowledge contained within its pages are timeless and have much to teach!

Finally, as art, Hasluck's manuals contain beautiful illustrations and line art that are a sign of simpler, yet authentic times when quality mattered and craftsmanship was king. This collectible volume makes a great addition to the bookshelf of any handcrafter, maker, artisan, farmer, homesteader, or outdoors enthusiast!

SMITHS' WORK

WITH NUMEROUS ENGRAVINGS AND DIAGRAMS

EDITED BY

PAUL N. HASLUCK

EDITOR OF "WORK" AND "BUILDING WORLD"
AUTHOR OF "HANDYBOOKS FOR HANDICRAFTS," ETC. ETC.

PHILADELPHIA
DAVID McKAY, Publisher
1022, MARKET STREET
1904

PREFACE.

This Handbook contains, in a form convenient for everyday use, a comprehensive digest of the knowledge of Smiths' Work, scattered over ten thousand columns of WORK—the weekly journal it is my fortune to edit—and supplies concise information on the general principles of the subjects on which it treats.

In preparing for publication in book form the mass of relevant matter contained in the volumes of WORK, much had to be arranged anew, altered, and largely re-written. From these causes the contributions of many are so blended that the writings of individuals cannot be distinguished for acknowledgment.

Readers who may desire additional information respecting special details of the matters dealt with in this Handbook, or instruction on kindred subjects, should address a question to WORK, so that it may be answered in the columns of that journal.

P. N. HASLUCK.

CONTENTS.

LIST OF ILLUSTRATIONS.

SMITHS' WORK.

CHAPTER I.

FORGES AND APPLIANCES.

IT is but fitting that the first chapter of a handbook on the art of the blacksmith should contain descriptions of the various appliances necessary to the performance of the work. The principal of these are noticed in this chapter, descriptions of the hand tools being given in the next chapter; descriptions of those appliances that require to be specially made for individual jobs are included in the explanations of the processes further on. Brief notices of some of the principal forges will be useful as a guide to the choice of one. Portable bellows forges, both rectangular and circular, are made in a great many sizes. One with a hearth measuring about 25 in. by 18 in. is sufficiently large for a single-handed worker, and in it bar iron up to 1 in. or $1\frac{1}{4}$ in. square may be heated. For heavier work, requiring the aid of a hammer-man, the hearth may measure 33 in. by 26 in., and range thence up to 39 in. by 30 in. for the largest work. The common forge built of bricks or stone is suitable for average and occasional heavy work.

The Sturtevant improved bench forge, Fig. 1, is of a very convenient height, and is especially adapted for light work. Fig. 2 illustrates a portable forge fitted with a long-shape bellows. The wrought-iron hooded forge, Fig. 3, has a circular blast bellows. Both of these latter forges are made and sold by Messrs. Linley & Bingham. Roots' patent "Acme" forge, as made by

Messrs. Samuelson & Co., Ltd., Banbury, is illustrated by Fig. 4. There is a cast-iron hearth to the forge shown on p. 13, though with other designs, hearths of wrought iron can be had.

Those who would prefer a gas forge may be interested in the sketch of one given in Fig. 5 ; it is built of angle iron, flat bars, and thin sheets.

For blast, a bellows, fan, or blower may be used.

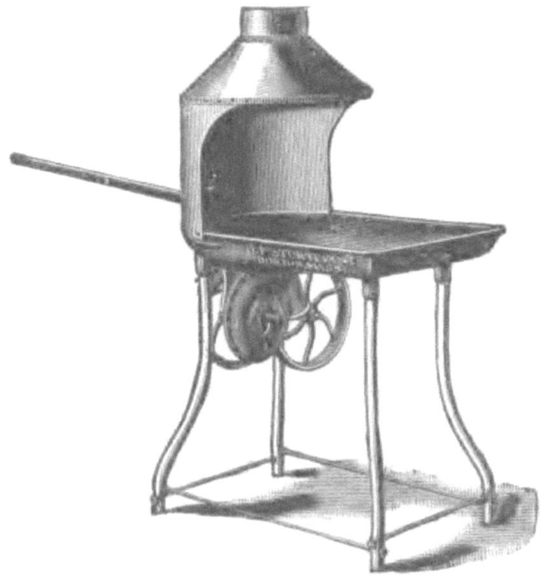

Fig. 1.—Sturtevant Improved Hand Forge.

A blower is undoubtedly the best; its equal and continuous blast is superior to the spasmodic variable, and intermittent current from bellows. There are several kinds of blowers used in portable forges, but there is not very much to choose between them. In workshops a row of forges will be supplied with blast from a single fan or blower, each forge being furnished with a throttle valve in its tuyere pipe. The old-fashioned bellows are still found in country shops; but in the modern establishments a fan blast or a blower is used, either being superior in all respects to the bellows. Preference should be given to a forge fitted with a blower of the Roots type, the construction of which is shown at Fig. 6.

A circular double-blast bellows, suitable for ordinary work, is illustrated by Fig. 7. It is made in sizes varying from 20 in. to 40 in., by Messrs. Linley & Bingham. Made

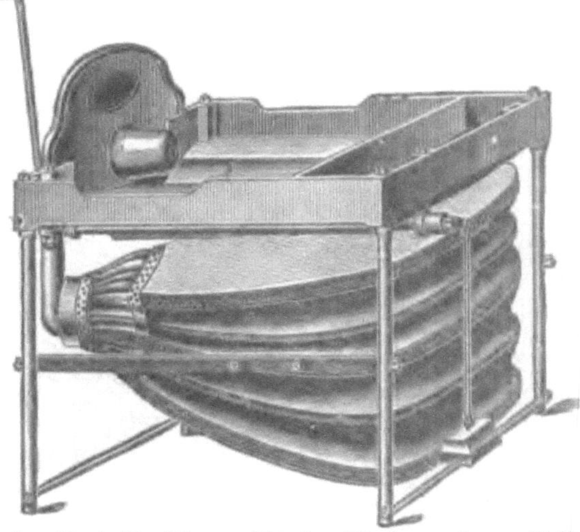

Fig. 2.—Portable Forge fitted with long-shape Bellows.

by the same firm is the smith's bellows shown in Fig. 8. This can be obtained in sizes varying from 24 in. to 42 in. long.

In small forges, the tuyere is a simple tube. The thickening-up of the nozzle serves to preserve it from destruction for a very long period, and the casting when burnt away is replaced. But in all large forges operated by powerful blast, the tuyere is surrounded with water, which protects the nose from the destructive heat of the fire. There are several forms of water tuyeres. The commonest are shown in Figs. 9 and 10. In Fig. 9 a cast-iron tank (A) contains water, which fills up the annular space (B) around the nozzle (C). In Fig. 10, which is made both in wrought and cast iron, a supply of water enters the annular space by the pipe (A) and leaves it by the pipe (B), so maintaining a constant circulation of water.

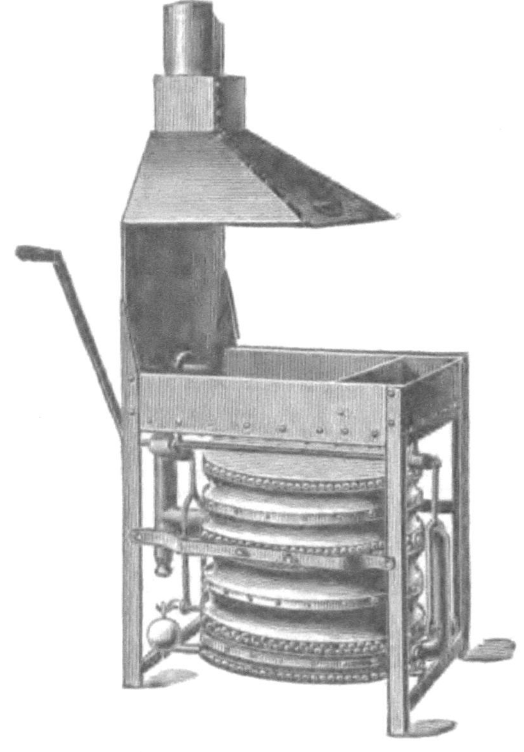

Fig. 3.—Wrought-iron Portable Forge, with Hood fitted with Circular Double-blast Bellows and Weight Balls.

Some idea as to the variety and arrangement of the tools and appliances used in smithing, is given by Figs. 11 and 12. In the former, Thwaite's fixed cast-iron hearth, together with anvil, hammers, cooling-trough, etc.. is shown ; whilst the latter illustrates a bench with its vice, a swage-block and stand, tongs, fullers, etc.

The London pattern anvil (Fig. 13) ranges in weight from about two to four cwt., and is made of steel-faced wrought iron. A double-piked anvil is shown by Fig. 14, and a farrier's anvil by Fig. 15. The conical end (A) or "beak" is used for turning bars upon, and the hole (B) is for the reception of the

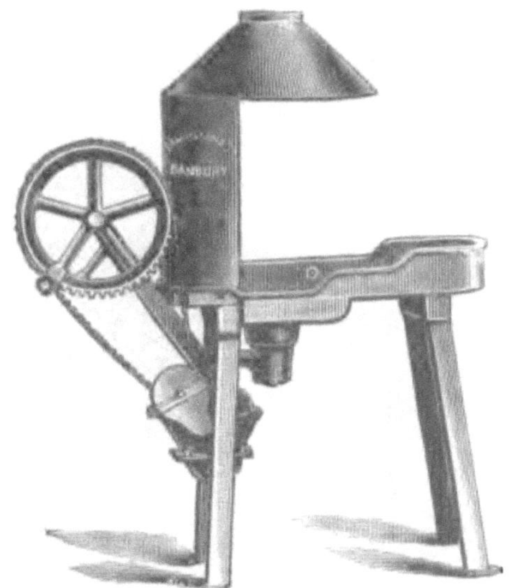

Fig. 4.—Roots' Patent "Acme" Forge.

anvil chisel, and various bottom tools. Care should be taken that the edges of the anvil are not bruised.

The anvil is supported so that its face is about 22 in. high from the ground by a stand which is often a block of wood. The anvil is prevented from slipping sideways by spikes driven into the wood close alongside the anvil-feet. An iron stand (Fig. 16) is much firmer than one of wood though its first cost is greater.

The anvil wears hollow on the surface in the course of time, and its edges become rounded; the less this occurs the better, as an anvil needs to be true when flatting over large surfaces and square corners. Occasionally, but very seldom, the beak is broken off, either as the result of faulty construction or very rough usage.

The ordinary tail or standing vice is, on the whole, as good as any. Vices with parallel jaws and instan-

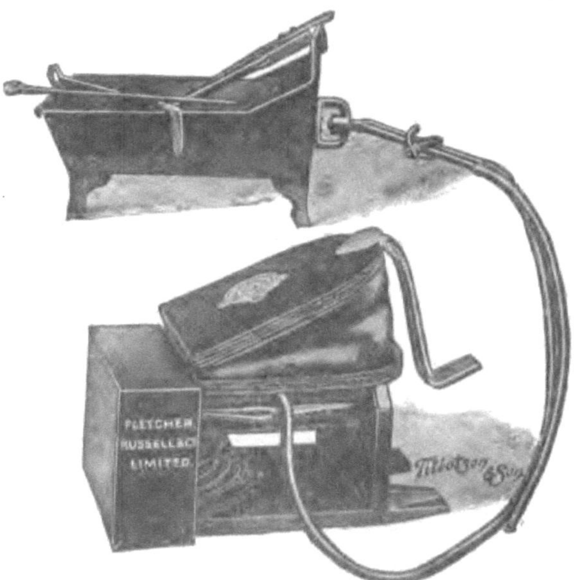

Fig. 5.—Fletcher, Russell & Co.'s Gas Forge.

taneous grip arrangements used by fitters are scarcely suitable for the smithy, where the work is mostly of a rough character. The tail-vice may be attached to a regular bench put up in the smithy, as shown in the general view, Fig. 12, on p. 20 ; or a small bench only two or three feet in length may be attached to the wall near the forge, and the vice fastened to that ; or it may be self-contained, standing on a tripod framework of wrought iron, and so be movable about the shop.

In a shop not provided with steam power, the Oliver hammer is a useful tool, and may easily and cheaply be rigged up by smith and carpenter; though not so rapid in its action as a steam-hammer, it is the best substitute for one. If power is available, the drop-hammer is an improvement on the Oliver, and is employed in many large firms. The steam-hammer is, however, the most efficient; but it consumes a large

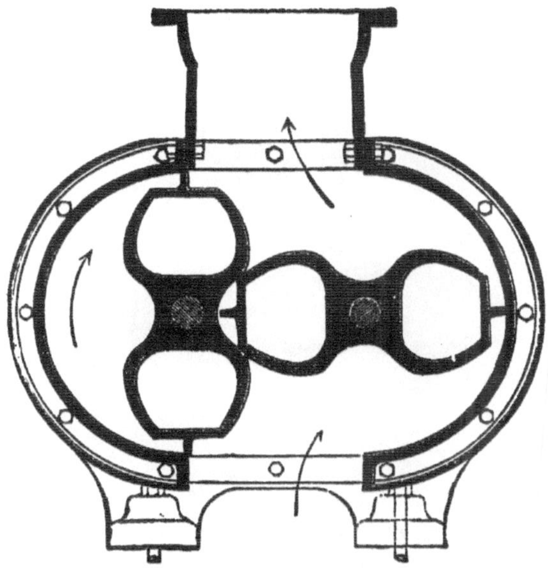

Fig. 6.—Section of Roots' Blower.

quantity of steam, requires the attendance of a man to operate the valves, is costly, and therefore only suitable to large shops.

Figs. 17 and 18 show a front and a side view of an Oliver hammer, as often fitted up in country shops, where the appliance is often entirely home made. A, A, are stout wooden posts driven deeply into the ground, between them being pivoted on dead centres a piece of wood, B, of either round or square section. Iron centres

are driven into the ends of B, and these are pivoted upon
studbolts, c, c. The pivots and the countersunk holes
should be case-hardened, and iron bands, D, D, should
be shrunk on to prevent the wood, B, being split out at
the ends. The hammer-shaft, E, is mortised into B, over
which, on each side of the hammer-shaft, bands, F, F, are
shrunk, to prevent the concussion of the hammer blows
splitting the wood. The hammer-head, G, is recessed as
shown, to receive top swages, and corresponding bottom
swages are let into the anvil, H, which, in turn, rests
upon a massive anvil-block, J.

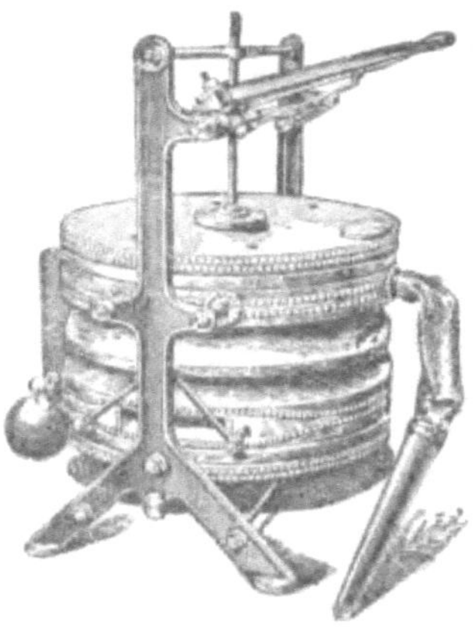

Fig. 7.—Circular Double-blast Bellows made in sizes
varying from 20 in. to 40 in.

The Oliver hammer is worked by the smith with
his foot upon the treadle-board, K, to which one end
of a chain L, is attached, the other end being fastened
to a flexible wooden pole, M. A short lever, N, is
fastened to the chain between K and M, and this
lever being driven into B, of which it forms a
part, moves B on its pivots and causes E and G to
descend with the treadle, K. On the release of the foot,
G is pulled up by the spring bar, M, which is tenoned
into a stout beam O, which is fastened to the wall.

There are several forms of drop hammers, a common arrangement being to attach the hammer to the lower end of a belt which is fastened to a pulley, the latter being revolved as required by friction cones, operated with a disengaging clutch. When the latter is released the hammer falls; on again throwing it into gear, the hammer is lifted. The clutch is controlled by means of a lever handle, within easy reach of the attendant.

A monkey or swinging pendulum hammer is illustrated by Fig. 19. It is made of cast iron, and is balanced carefully on its centre of gravity by the correct setting in position of the eye B, which is cast into the bar. The battering end is preserved from fracture, and from too rapid wear, by means of the wrought iron band C which fits around, and is shrunk into a shouldered recess of dovetailed section. The handle, or porter, D is of wrought iron cast into the monkey. It is provided with an eye, through which a small chain or rope E is passed; by means of this the monkey is pulled backwards after every blow. The monkey is suspended by a chain A from any convenient beam overhead. It is drawn back several feet from the perpendicular, and then

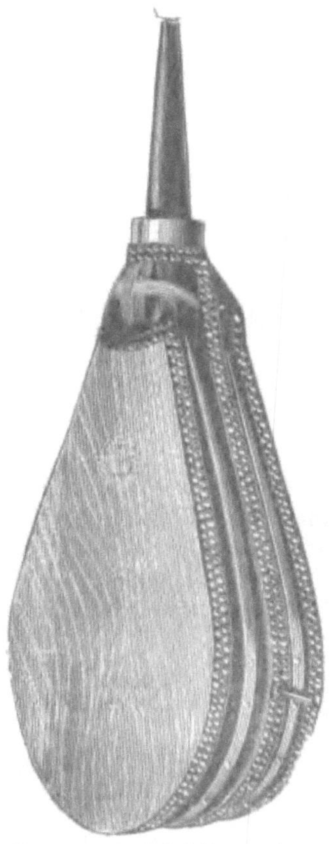

Fig. 8.—Smiths' Long-shape Bellows, extra leathered and double nailed. In sizes varying from 24 in. to 42 in.

let go; being heavy it strikes the iron with great force.

The smith's mandrel, Fig. 20, a conical hollow cast-

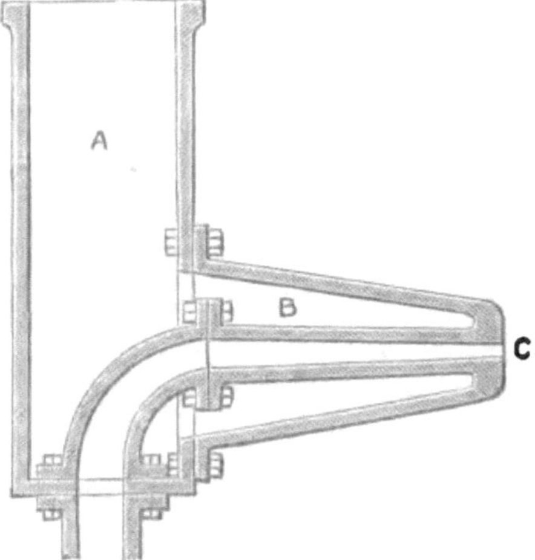

Fig. 9.—Tank Water Tuyere.

ing, is employed chiefly in making rings, as will be explained, and should be kept in three or four sizes.

An appliance employed for rounding off the heads of bolts is shown in plan and elevation by Figs. 21 and 22. A

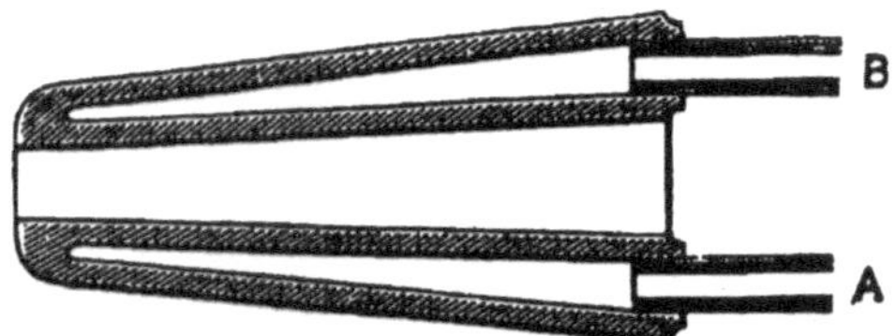

Fig. 10.—Pipe Water Tuyere.·

is a bracket-like casting, bolted firmly to a heavy cast-iron base let into the ground. Through an overhanging boss at the top of A slides the shank of the rounding tool, B. This is plumb over a bolster, c, on the base.   The bolt is dropped into the bolster, c, and the tool, B, struck upon it with a sledge hammer. The support, D, is

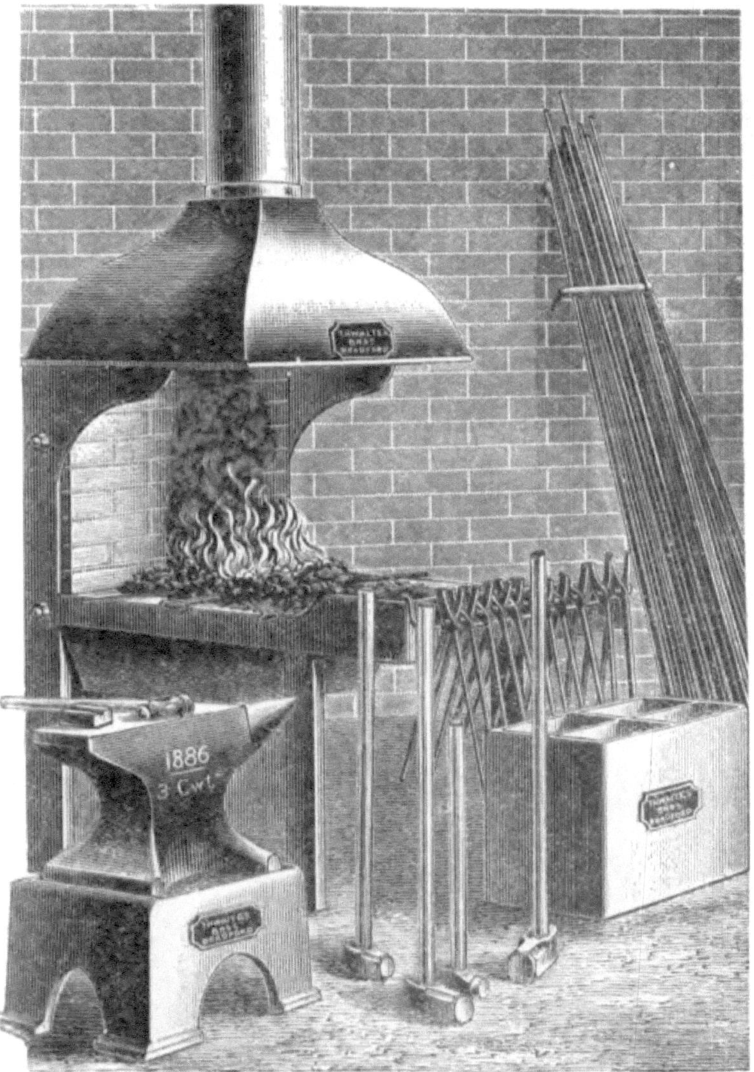

Fig. 11.—Smithy Forge.

merely for the purpose of supporting the rounding tool
while the bolt is being slipped into the bolster.   It is

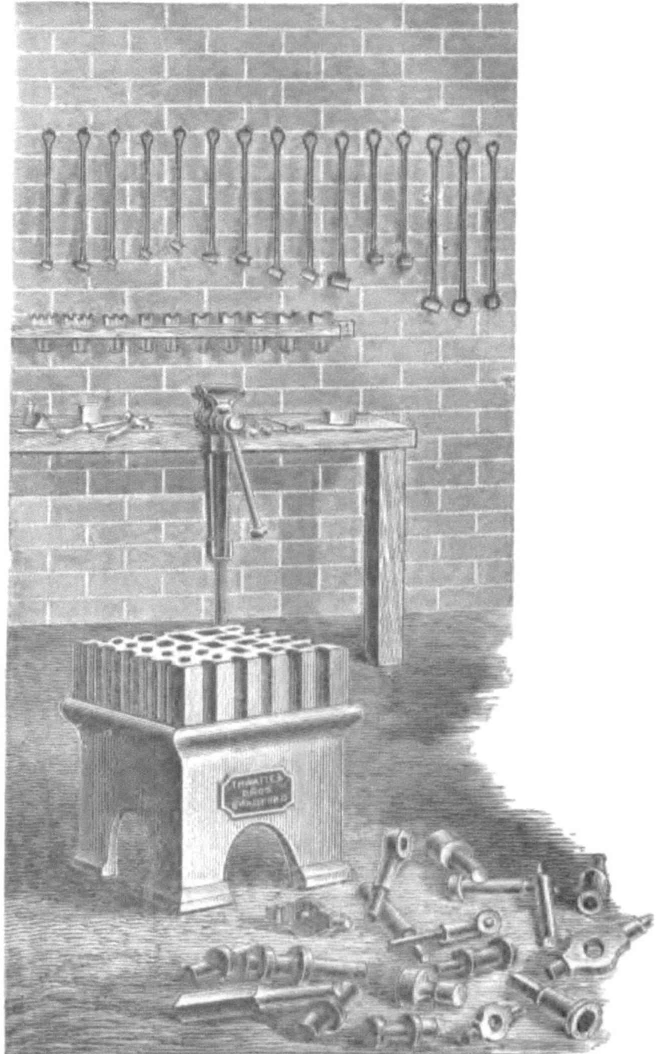

Fig. 12.—Smithy Bench.

pivoted to a strap fastened to the side of A, and is turned to one side when the tool is being struck with the hammer

A bolt-forging machine is power-driven, and by its means bolts and their heads are formed between dies

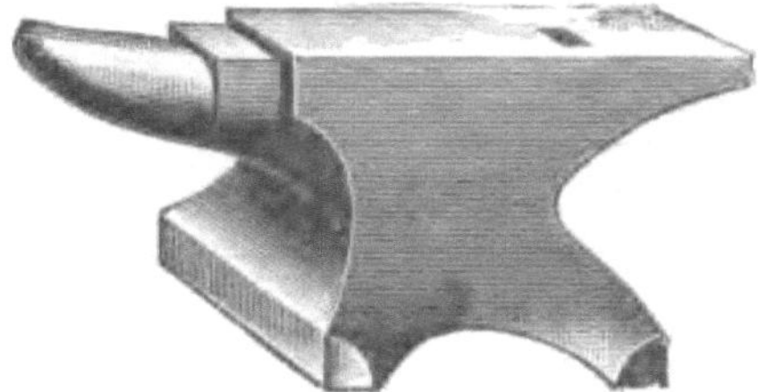

Fig. 13.—London Pattern Anvil.

having a rapid vertical movement imparted from a long cam shaft. Where bolts are made in even moderate

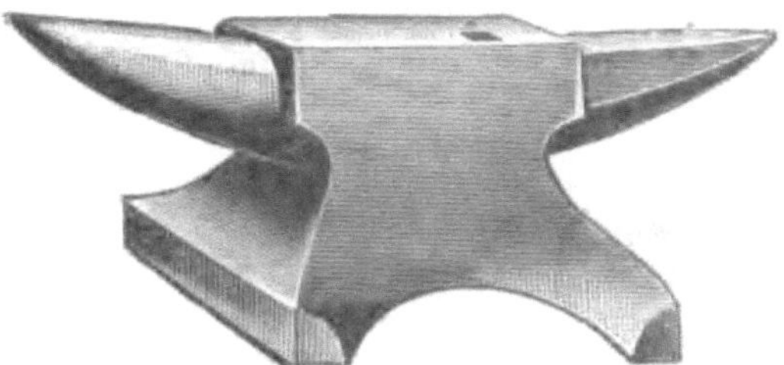

Fig. 14.—Double Piked Anvil.

quantities, the bolt-machine soon pays for itself. An almost necessary adjunct to this machine is the power-

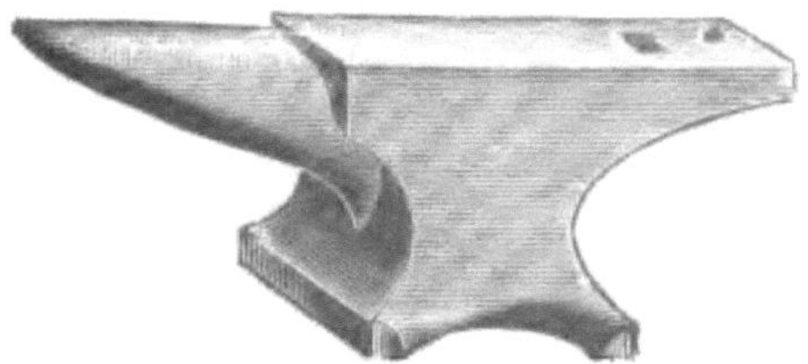

Fig. 15.—Farrier's Anvil.

driven hot and cold iron saws. The first is a comparatively thin saw, run dry at a high rate of speed, that cuts roughly through red-hot rods and bars almost instantly. The second is a thicker saw, that cuts slowly, but smoothly and cleanly, running in water the while.

Two forms of carriers are commonly employed to

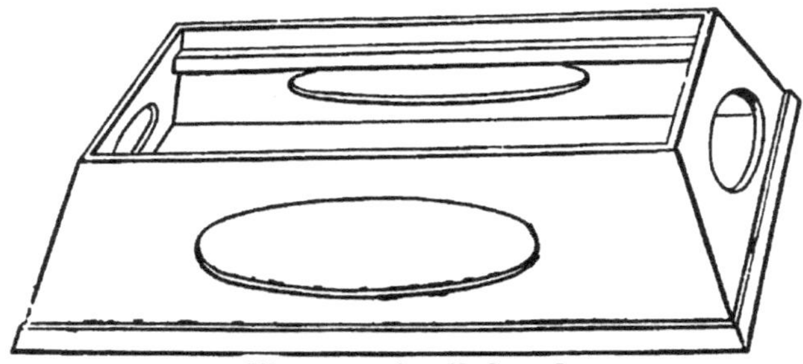

Fig. 16.—Anvil Stand.

move and carry about bars which are too long to be manipulated by the tongs.   One (Fig. 23) is used

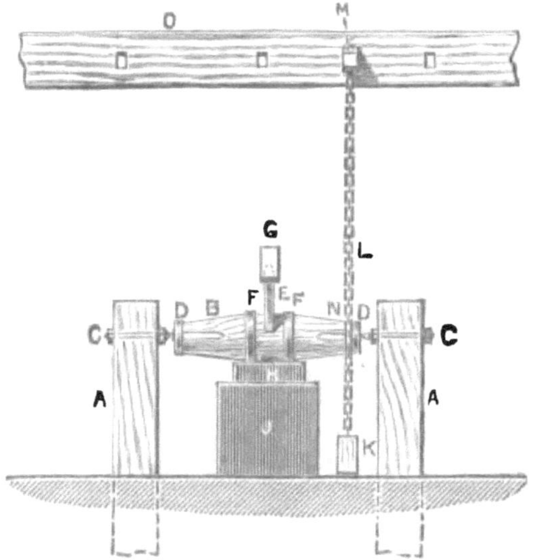

Fig. 17.—Front of Oliver Hammer.

underhand, being carried vertically with the hook lowermost, and the work, or one end of it, slung in the hook.   The other (Fig. 24) is used for heavy forgings, being carried by two men. When one end of the work is carried thus, the other may be slung in the crane, or

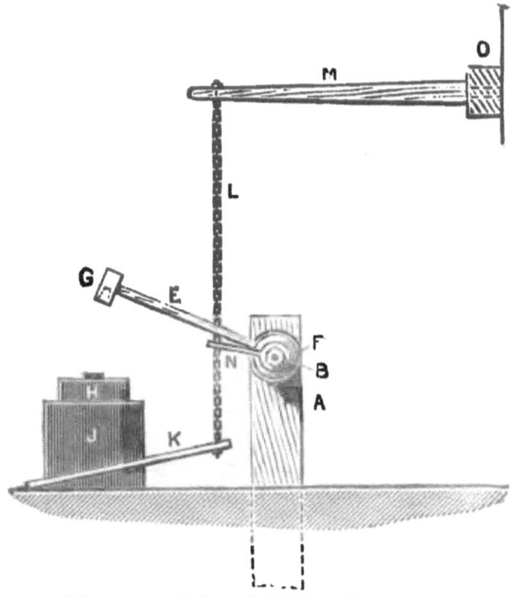

Fig. 18.—Side of Oliver Hammer.

be merely supported with the tongs, or balanced by other means.

Long rods and bars, when being cut off or welded,

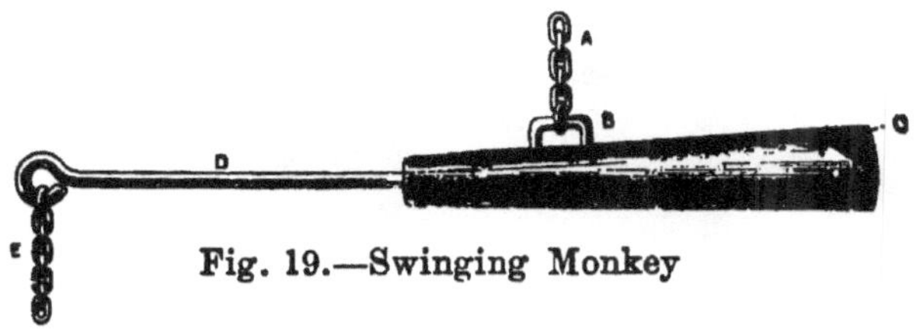

Fig. 19.—Swinging Monkey

require some support at the end farthest away from the smith. Support is also wanted when two rods are being welded by a single-handed worker; one rod is held by the smith but the other has to be supported by some mechanical contrivance, which should be provided with some means of adjusting the height, to suit differences in the bulk or thickness of the work.

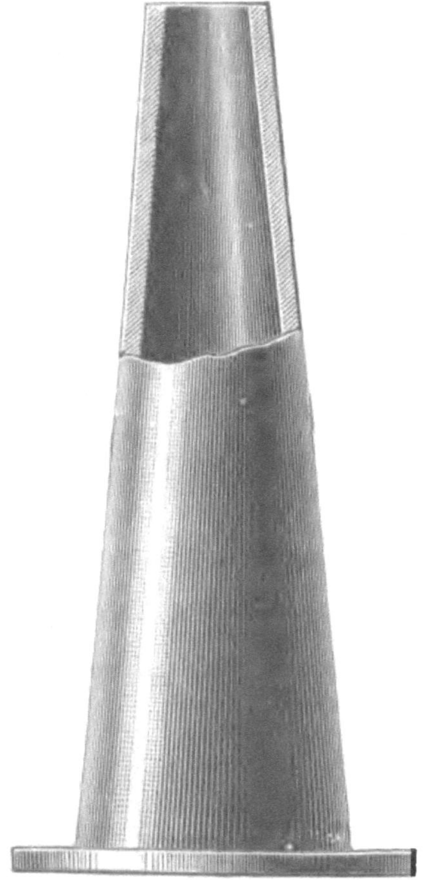

Fig. 20.—Sugar-loaf Casting.

Contrivances of this kind are shown in Figs. 25 and 26, and both, of course, are portable. In the one shown by Fig. 25, two cheeks, A, of wrought iron, cut to the outline shown in the end view, and maintained at a definite distance apart with the stay bolts, B, B, are pierced with numerous holes, C, at different heights. Into any of these holes the bolt, D, can be inserted, carrying the loose roller, E, that supports the work.

In the second contrivance (Fig. 26), two uprights, A, are tenoned into a foot, B. Between the uprights the forked piece, C, slides, and by the insertion of pins, D D, in any pair of the series of holes in the uprights the height of the fork, and consequently of the work, is regulated.

Sometimes the support consists simply of a forked end screwed into a socket, and turned up or down with the hand ; the adjustment of this appliance is more exact than in the others.

Another method of supporting heavy work is by means of an endless sling chain dependent from a loose pulley, slung from a light jib overhead. This contrivance is often used simply for lifting work of considerable bulk from the fire to the anvil and back

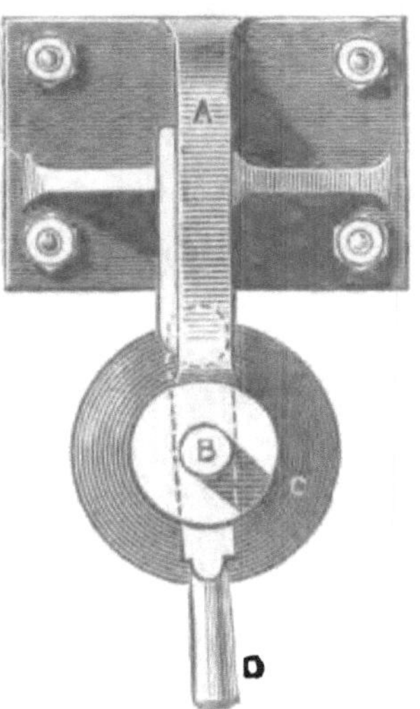

Fig. 21.—Plan of Appliance for Rounding Bolt Heads.

again. For heavier work a pair of pulley blocks are often slung from a jib, and then there is mechanical gain, and facility for raising and lowering the work as well.

Fig. 27 shows a simple and effective rig-up for manipulating heavy work. Use is made of the movable jib, which is an accessory to most forges. It is pivoted against the wall, and upon its cheeks, A, A, runs the jenny, B, consisting of four wheels and carriage, with a depending hook, C, to which is attached a lever having a long arm, D, and a short arm, E. At the end of the short arm is a square nut, F, threaded to take a coarse, square-threaded screw, G, which passes up clear by the

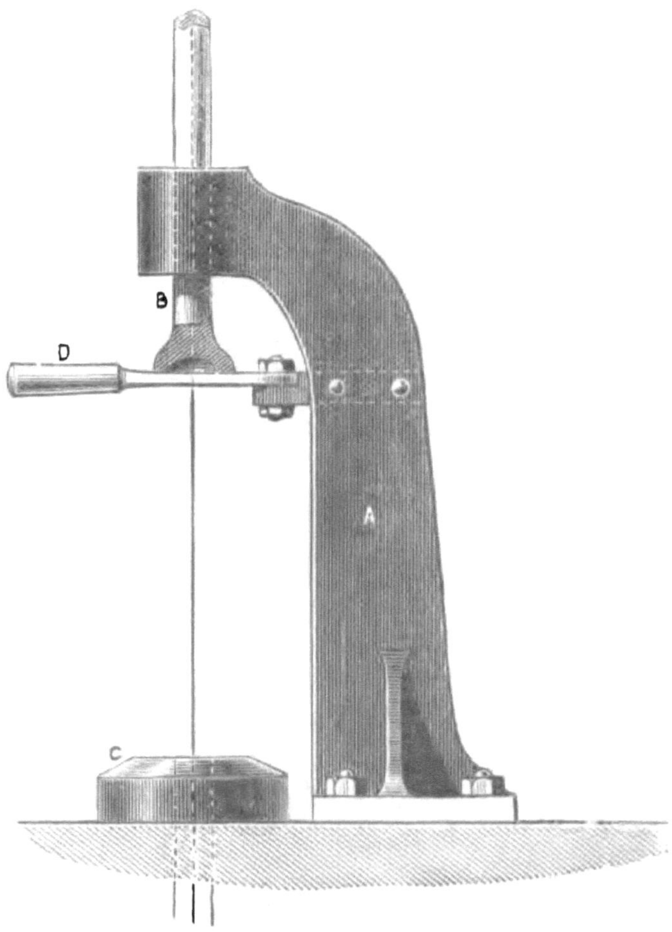

Fig. 22.—Elevation of Appliance for Rounding Bolt Heads.

side of the crane.   At the lower end of this screw is a swivel, H, through which the screw works, being turned by a lever passing through the hole in the boss at the

lower end of the screw, G. From the lower end of the
swivel depends the chain and clip in which the work is

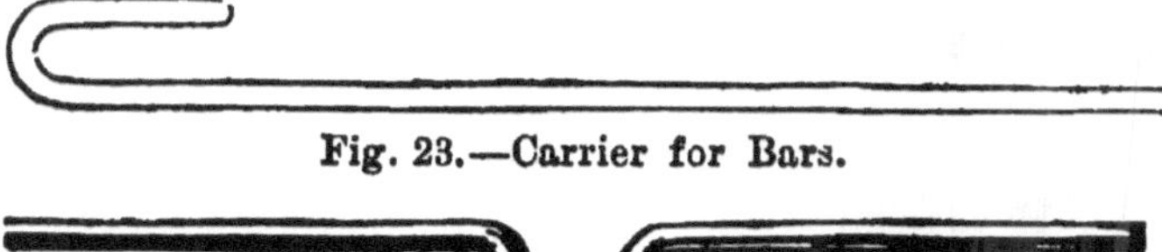

Fig. 23.—Carrier for Bars.

Fig. 24.—Carrier for Bars.

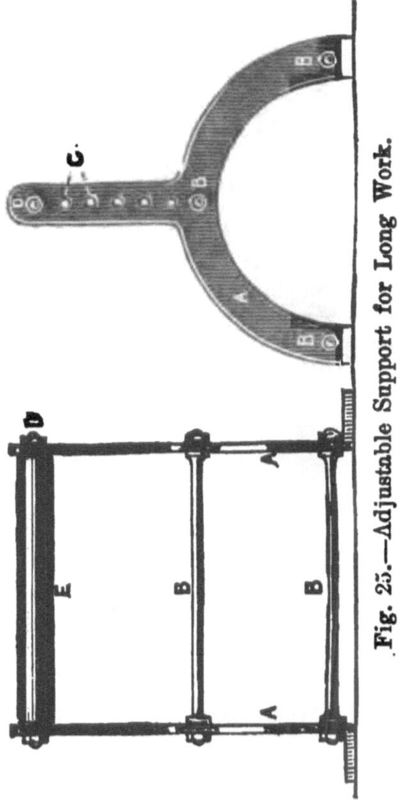

Fig. 25.—Adjustable Support for Long Work.

suspended. Adjustment of the height of the work
can be made by turning the screw, G, the range of

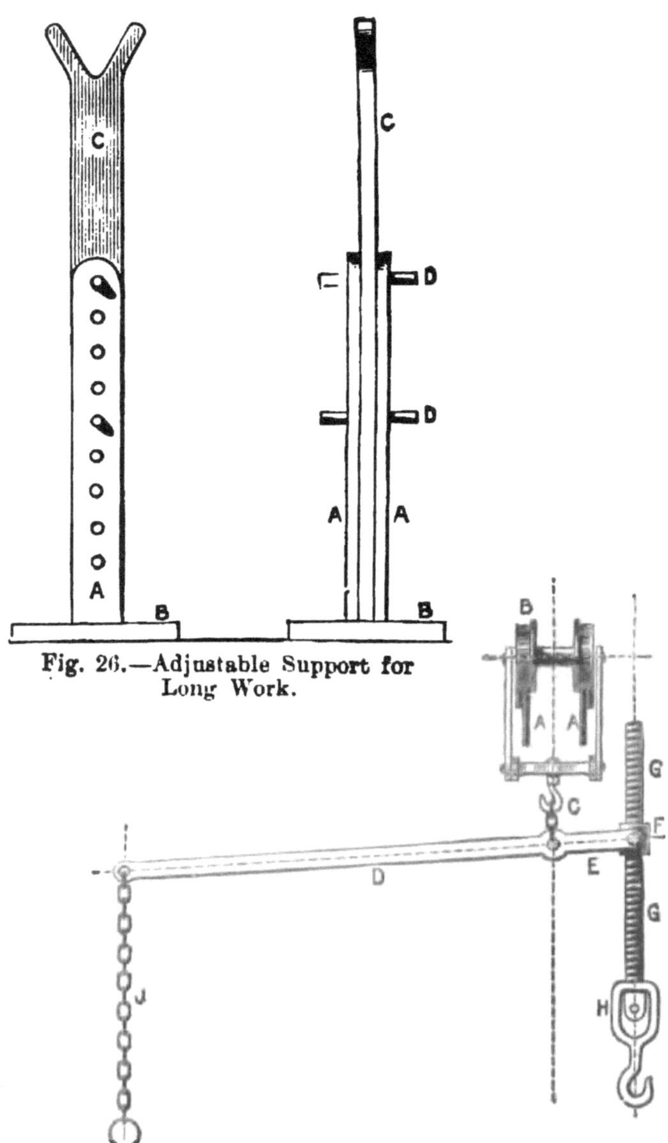

Fig. 26.—Adjustable Support for
Long Work.

Fig. 27.—Apparatus for Lifting Heavy Forgings.

height being equal to the length of the screw, and by pulling at the chain, J, at the long end of the lever. This latter being rapid and immediate in action, is used during the manipulation of the work. The exercise of very little force, such as a man can apply with one hand, is sufficient to raise and lower the work upon the anvil or the bending block, and to move it to any position required.

CHAPTER II

HAND TOOLS.

THE smith's miscellaneous small hand tools, though numerous, consist mostly of appliances for moulding or shaping metal into diverse forms. Like the tools

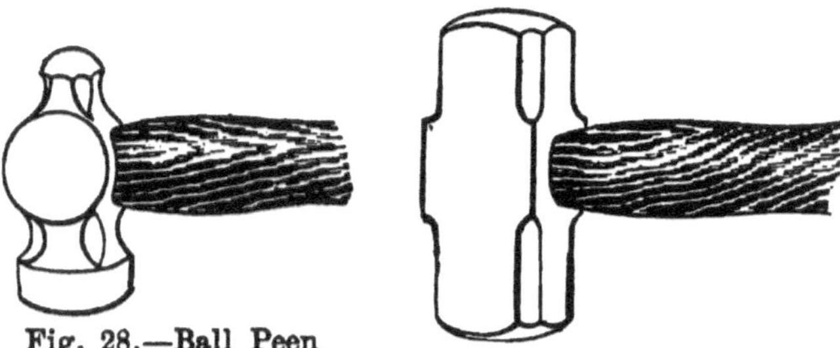

Fig. 28.—Ball Peen Hammer.

Fig. 29.—Sledge Hammer.

used in some other trades, many are made as occasion requires, and accumulate quickly.

The smith's hammers, other than power driven, are of two kinds—the hand hammer and the sledge. The

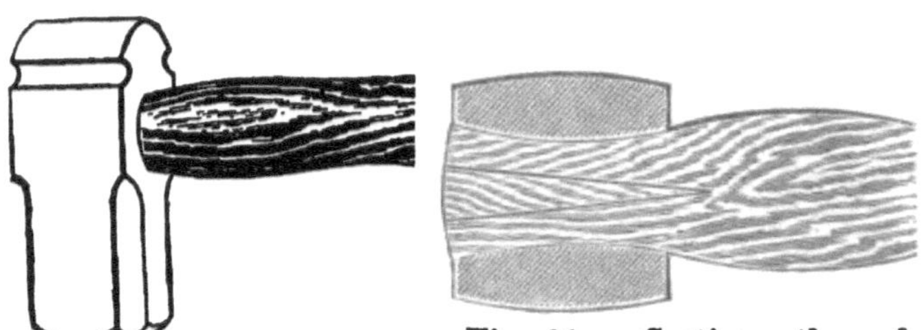

Fig. 30.—Sledge Hammer.

Fig. 31. — Section through Wedged Hammer Head.

first-named weighs from $\frac{1}{2}$ lb. to 1 lb., and generally is of the form shown in Fig. 28, with the ball peen. The cross peen hand hammer is used for fullering and drawing down. The flat face is used for striking heavy blows and for finishing surfaces. The sledges

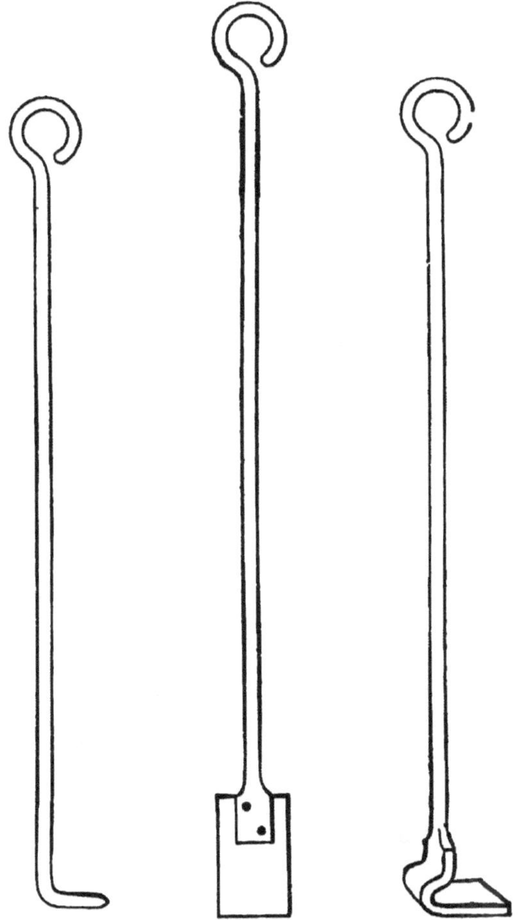

Fig. 32.—Poker. Fig. 33.—Slice. Fig. 34.—Rake.

are of one of the two forms shown in Figs. 29 and 30, and weigh from 4 to 14 lb., one of from 6 to 8 lb. weight being about the average. Fig. 31 shows the method of wedging on the head to prevent it from flying off. Hammer handles should be kept in a dry place for several weeks previous to use; if they are

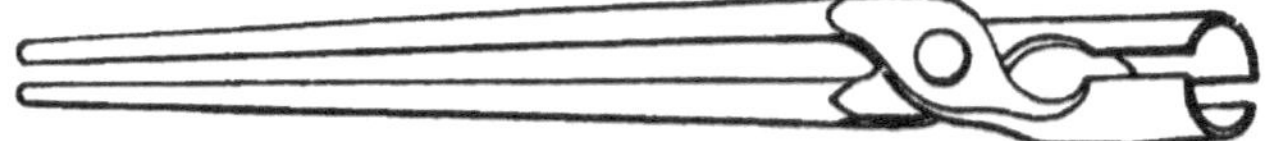

Fig. 35.—Hollow Bit Tongs.

not well seasoned, they shrink with the heat and are apt to work loose on their heads.

The necessary firing tools are the poker, Fig. 32,

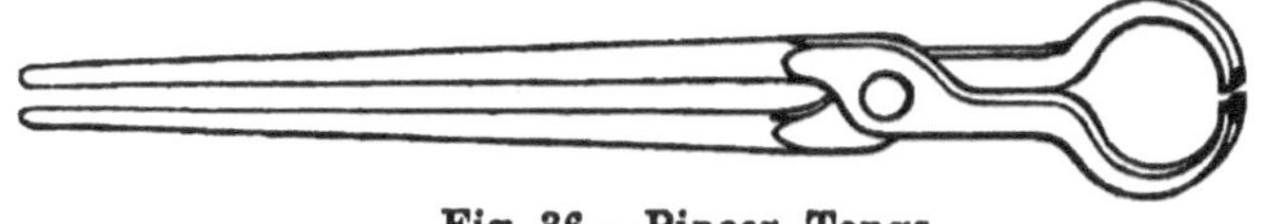

Fig. 36.—Pincer Tongs.

the slice, Fig. 33, and the rake, Fig. 34. Their uses are obvious.

Before any forging can be done tongs are necessary

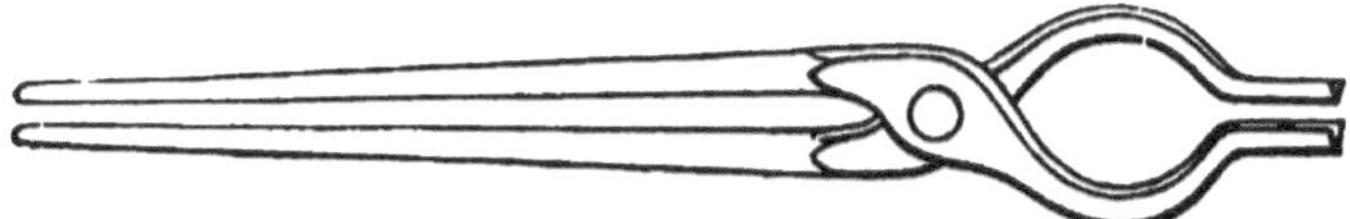

Fig. 37.—Tongs with V-shaped Jaws.

There are often a dozen tongs to a moderately well-appointed forge, but it is not necessary to get them all at once; a few of the simpler and most necessary

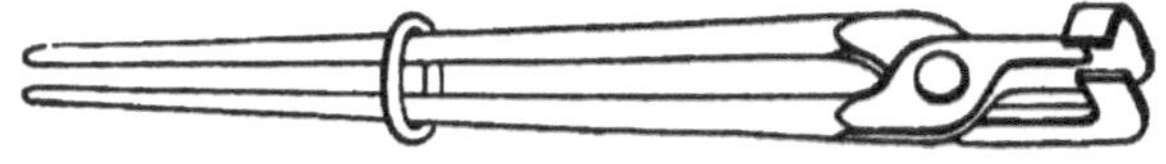

Fig. 38.—Crook Bit Tongs.

tongs will now be described. Each of these tools is made in several sizes to suit the various kinds of work.

Fig. 35 shows the hollow-bit tongs; enclosing and gripping the rod for a length of about 2 in., they take a very firm hold of both rods and bars. When there is a collar or other enlargement at one end of a bar, the pincer tongs, Fig. 36, are sometimes employed to enable a firm grip to be taken ; the jaws have V-notches, as shown in the end view. Fig. 37 shows

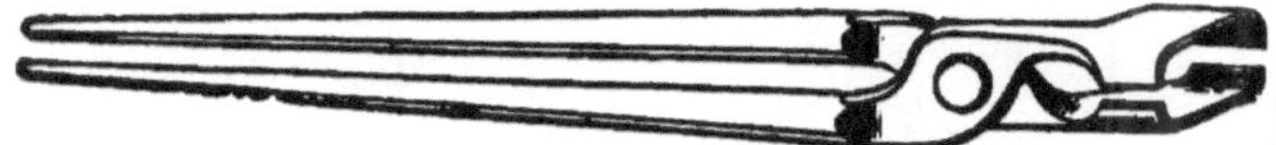

Fig. 39.—Tongs for Flat Bars.

tongs that are more generally useful; the elongation of the V-shaped jaws gives a stronger grip, and the rod or bar is less liable to shift sideways.

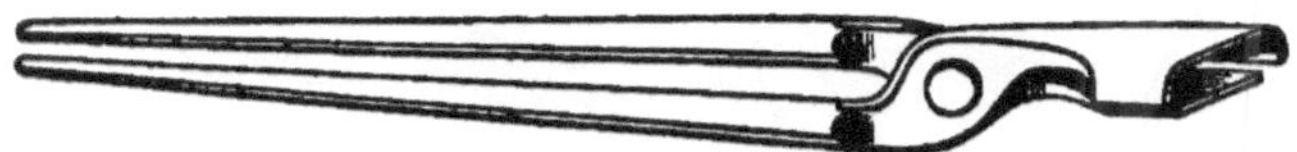

Fig. 40.—Tongs for Flat Bars.

When a bar is so long that it cannot be held with these tongs, a crook-bit tongs (Fig. 38) is used ; the jaws being turned aside permits the bar to pass along-

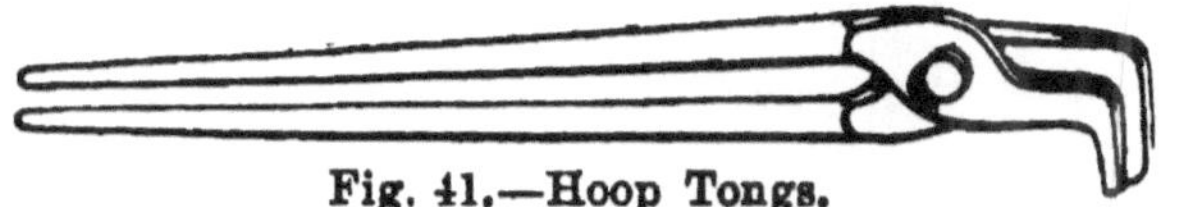

Fig. 41.—Hoop Tongs.

side the handles on one side of the rivet. The lip serves to retain the bar in place, otherwise it would be apt to slip out sideways. With these four kinds

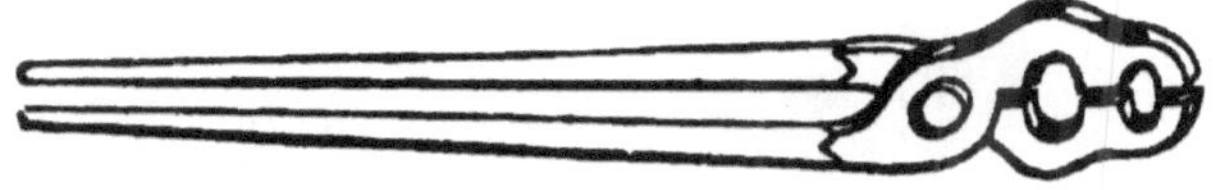

Fig. 42.—Pick-up Tongs.

of tongs work can be commenced on round rods and square bars of iron. For other work there are other forms. The ring encircling the handles or reins of the crook-bit tongs is called a coupler, which is slid over the reins, and tightened by a tap or two with the hammer

c

The work is thus grasped without the need of any further effort on the part of the smith.

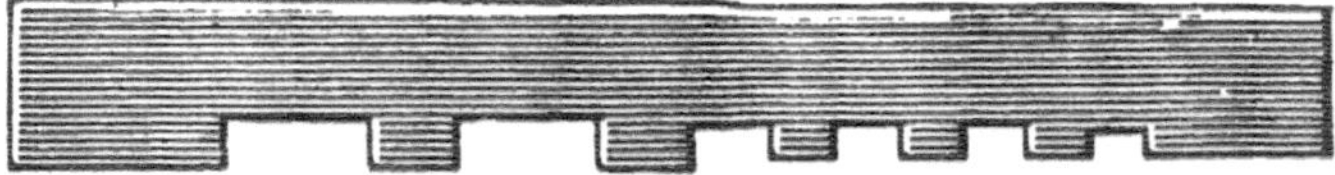

Fig. 43.—Gap Gauge.

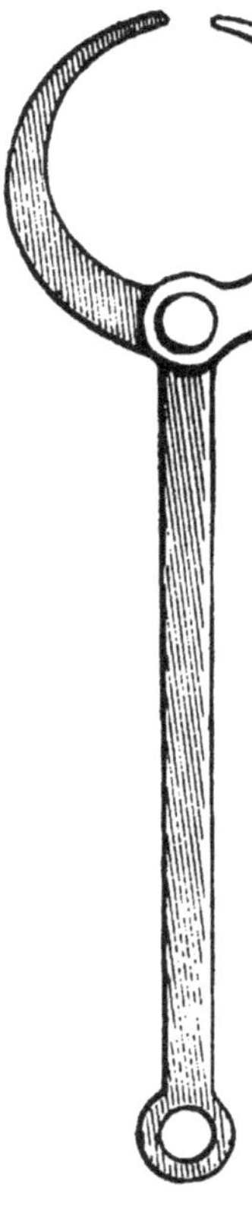

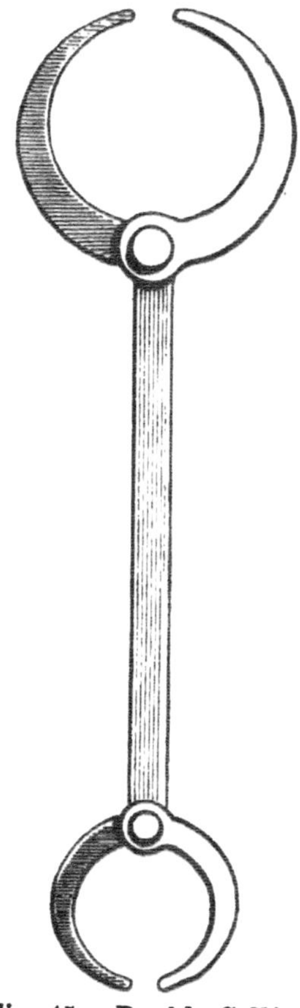

Fig. 44.—Single Calliper. Fig. 45.—Double Callipers.

For holding flat bars, tongs shaped like those shown at Figs. 39 and 40 are employed. In Fig. 39 the jaws are alike, and come into direct opposition. In Fig. 40 a flat jaw falls within the sides of the other. These are made in various widths and proportions, the range of each pair being rather limited. For holding and

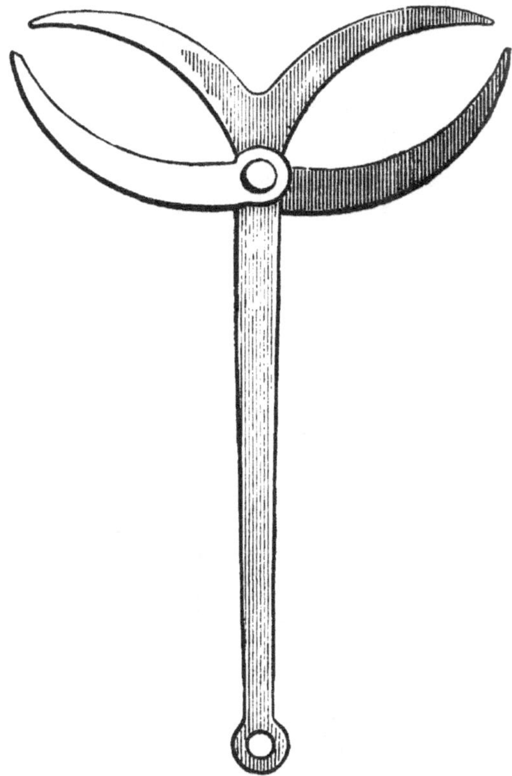

Fig. 46.—Double Callipers.

manipulating rings, hoop tongs (Fig. 41) and pick-up tongs (Fig. 42) are employed.

When work is being reduced to final dimensions, it is necessary to check sizes by tools other than the steel rule. For flat rods the gap gauge is commonly used. It is of the typical form shown in Fig. 43, each gap being of a definite width and differing from its neighbour by $\frac{1}{8}$ in. or $\frac{1}{16}$ in. Their depth is unimportant, but bears some proportion to width. These

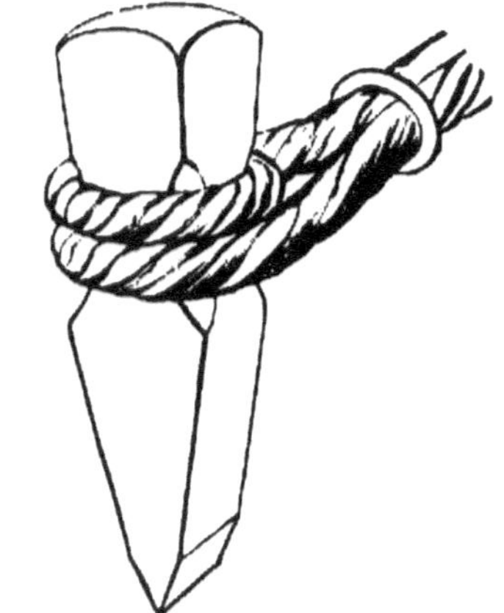

Fig. 47.—Cold Set.

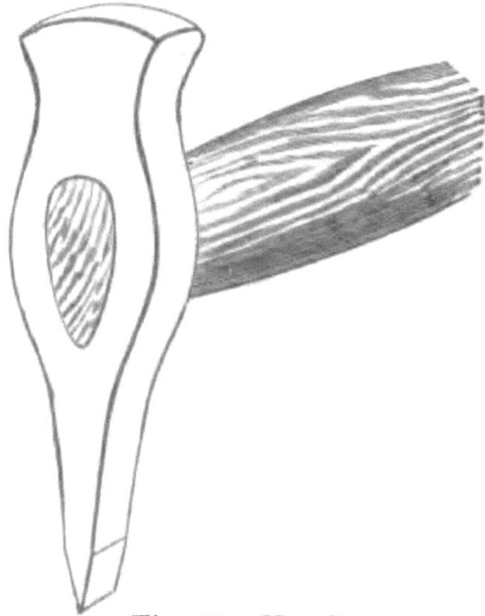

Fig. 48.—Hot Set.

gaps, which are really fixed calipers, can be used in an instant to embrace and test the dimensions of a red-hot forging.

For circular work calipers with long shanks are used. Fig. 44 shows a single caliper, whilst Figs. 45 and 46 are two forms of double calipers.

To cut a cold bar, it is nicked round with a cold set (Fig. 47). The bar is laid across the anvil with the chisel-edge upon it, and the chisel, being struck with a hammer, nicks the bar. The bar is rotated slightly and another blow struck, and so on rapidly

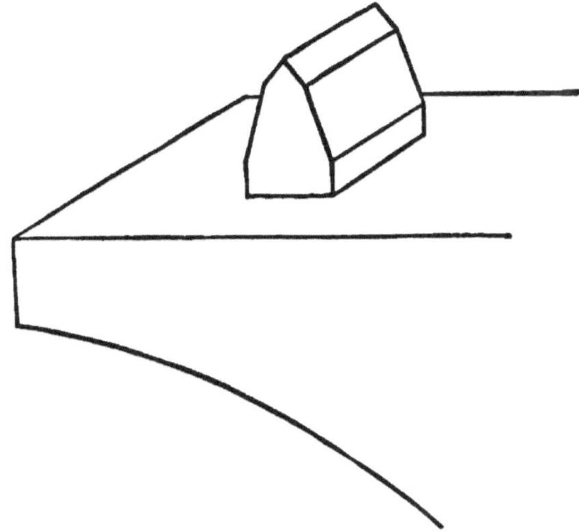

Fig. 49.—Anvil Cutter.

until there is a sharp indentation all round the bar. Then it is struck sharply across the edge of the anvil and snapped in two at the nicked section.

A hot-set (Fig. 48) is used if a bar is divided while red-hot, and the smith holds it in place while the hammer-man strikes it. The set is driven in deeply, and several blows are given at one spot; and by the time the bar has been turned completely round the set has almost or entirely severed it. In use the set becomes hot, so that it would be liable to lose its temper and become soft; therefore, after every four or five blows on the hot iron, the smith dips it into water to cool it.

The hot sets are often provided with handles differing

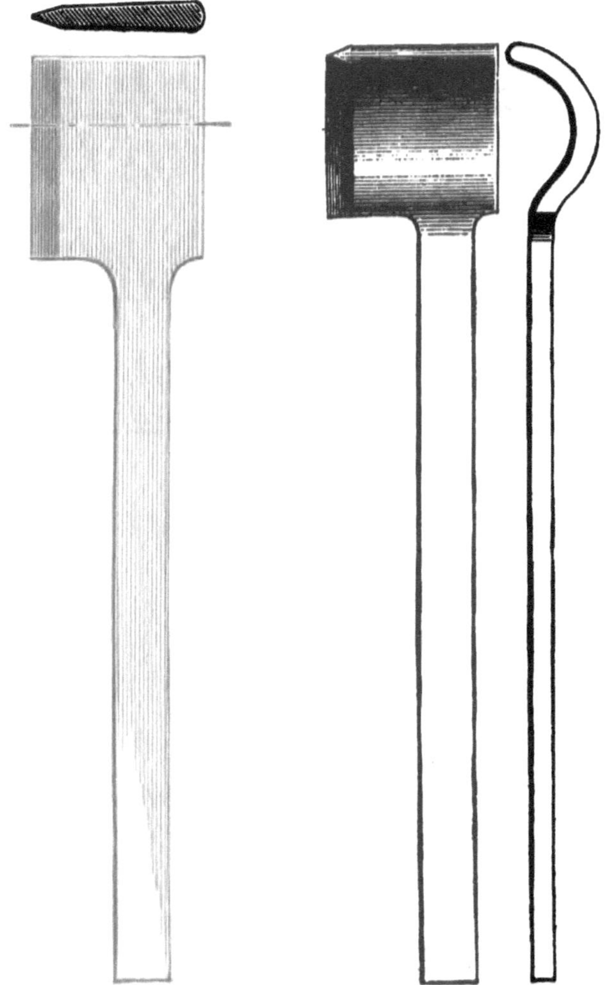

Fig. 50.—Chisel for Cutting   Fig. 51.—Chisel for Cutting
Iron Bars.   Circular Ends.

from those of the swages ; that is, they are like hammers,
but without wedges, which would shrink and become

loose, because they are subjected to more heat. When the handle becomes loose, striking its butt end upon

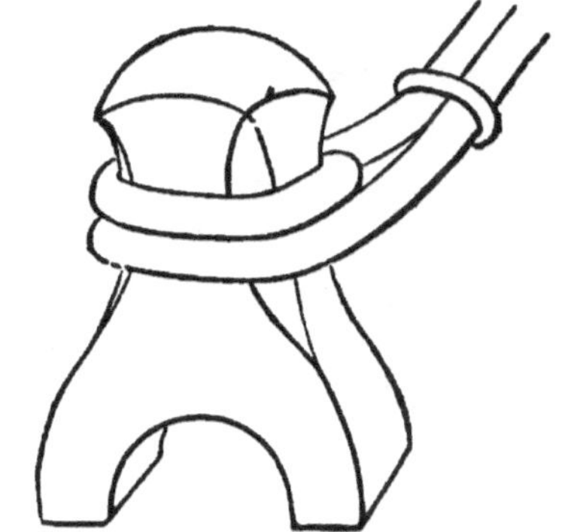

Fig. 52.—Top Swage.

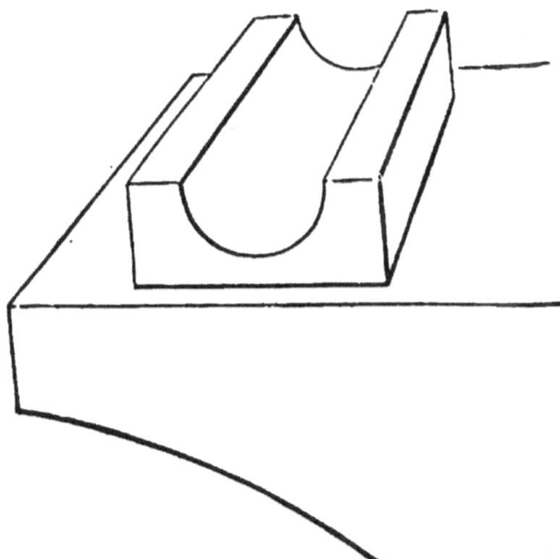

Fig. 53.—Bottom Swage.

the anvil jumps the set down to a firm hold, ready for immediate use. Sometimes they are provided with iron handles, or with withy handles as shown in Fig. 47.

A smith working single-handed when nicking bars uses the anvil cutter (Fig. 49). It is essentially a chisel, having its edge uppermost and a shank fitting into the square hole in the anvil; a bar laid upon it and struck with the hammer is nicked on the under side,

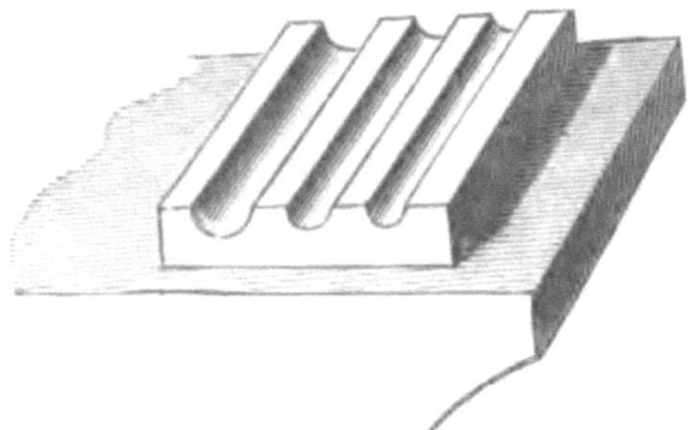

Fig. 54.—Bottom Swage.

and rotating and striking it with the hammer will have the effect of nicking it all round.

The knife tool, Fig. 50, and the curved tool, Fig. 51, are used for cutting lengths off iron bars.

Swages of many shapes are used for a variety of

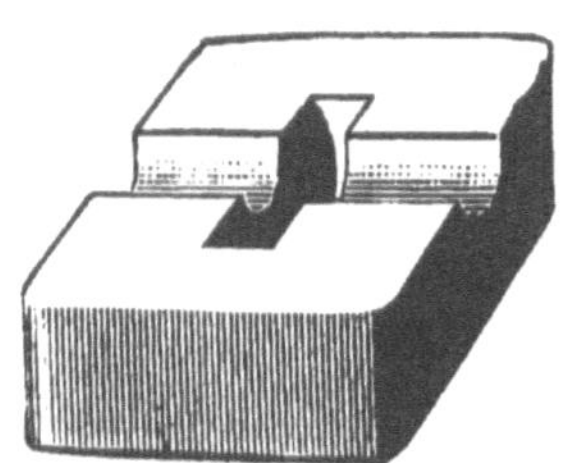

Fig. 55.—Swage for Collars.

purposes which will be duly explained. Top and bottom swages are illustrated respectively by Figs. 52 and 53.

A bottom swage like Fig. 54 is very useful, both for bolt making and for general work. Using this, a gradual reduction in diameter can be made without the trouble of changing the separate single bottom swages. A swage for finishing collars is illustrated by Fig. 55.

In the spring swages, Figs. 56, 57, and 58, the top swages guide themselves, and the work can be held in position and hammered to shape by one operator. The difference between the three is that, whilst Figs. 56 and 57 each take one diameter of iron, Fig. 58 will take three different sizes. The top and bottom faces of two, it will be noted, are made flat for use with the

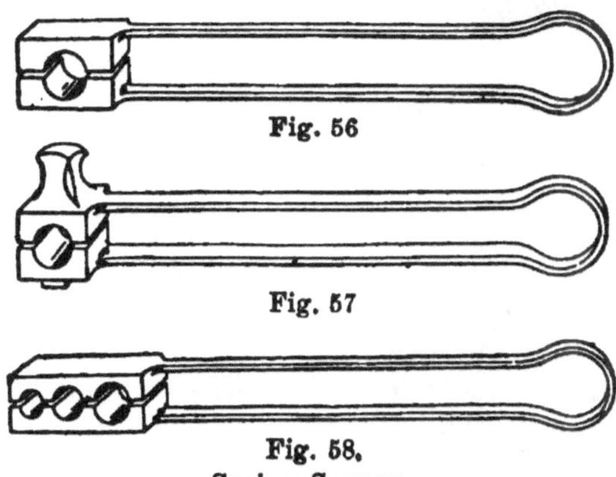

Fig. 56

Fig. 57

Fig. 58.
Spring Swages.

hammer, while in Fig. 57 the lower swage has a pin to fit into the anvil, and the upper swage is formed to be struck with the sledge-hammer.

The angular swage, Fig. 59, is used in shaping and welding hot metal. The angles support the sides of the metal whilst being hammered, and the work is performed more quickly—an important matter in welding. With this tool, a top swage can be used if desired, or the sledge or steam hammer by itself. In Figs. 60 and 61, similar swages are shown as forming bolt heads.

The common swage block, Fig. 62, is an appliance without which no smith's outfit is fairly complete. Its body is pierced with numerous holes—round, square, and oblong—and its edges are provided with grooves of various sizes, in circular and V forms. The block is used lying on its side, as a bolster, upon which holes are punched and drifted, and as a heading-tool, upon which shouldered work is finished. When laid upon one of its edges, the grooves serve as bottom swages for circular, hexagonal, and rectangular work.

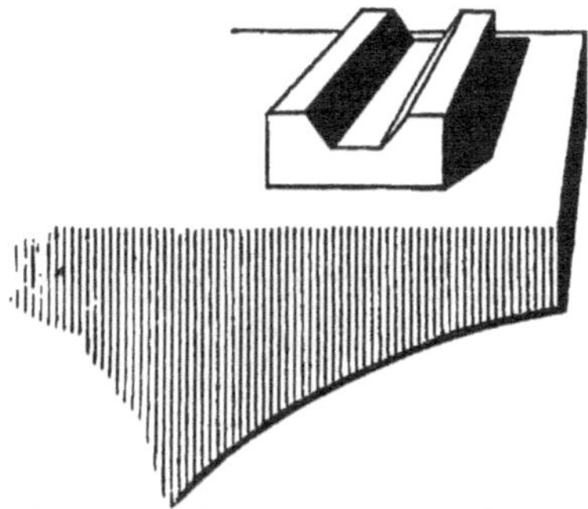

Fig. 59.—Nut Swage on Anvil.

The stand upon which the swage block is mounted may consist of upper and lower cast-iron frames, with the upper one provided with strips, enclosing the block. The two frames are held together by four shouldered wrought-

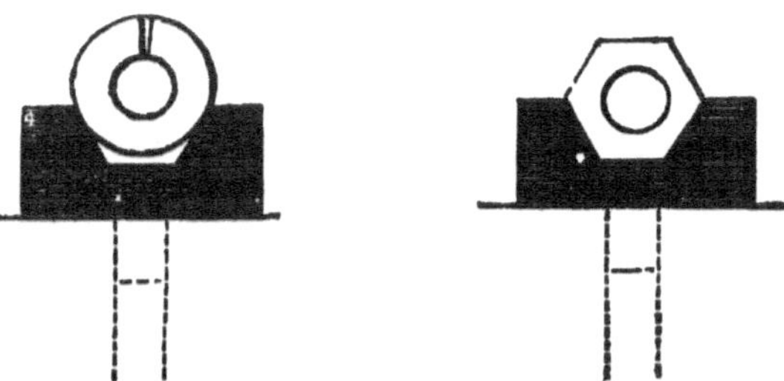

Fig. 60.—Bolt Head Laid in Bottom Tool.

Fig. 61.—Bolt Head Shaped in Bottom Tool.

iron pillars, whose pins pass through holes cast in the frames, and are riveted over at top and bottom. Fig. 63 shows a stand.

An essential tool is the fuller, of which four forms are here illustrated; Fig. 64 shows an ordinary top fuller, Fig. 65 the bottom fuller, Fig. 66 the round-faced fuller, and Fig. 67 the hollow fuller.　Another form of hollow tool is shown by Fig. 68 as finishing a ring on a **V**-block.　These tools enter into much of the

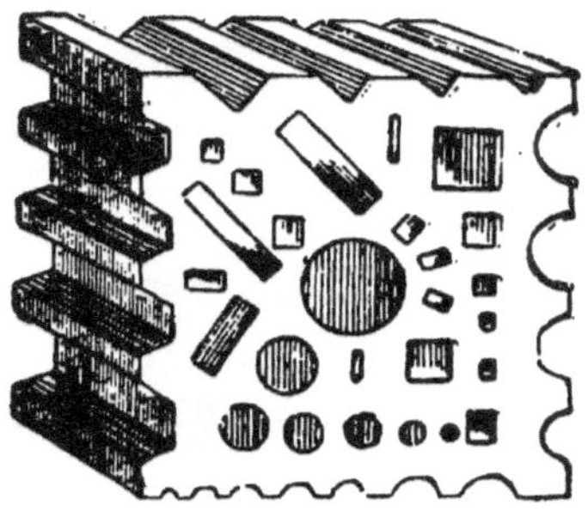

Fig. 62.—Swage Block.

smith's work, as will be made apparent as the subject is pursued.

The flatter, Fig. 69, is held by the smith whilst the hammermen strike it with sledges.　The cup tool, Fig. 70, is used in the same manner as the flatter.

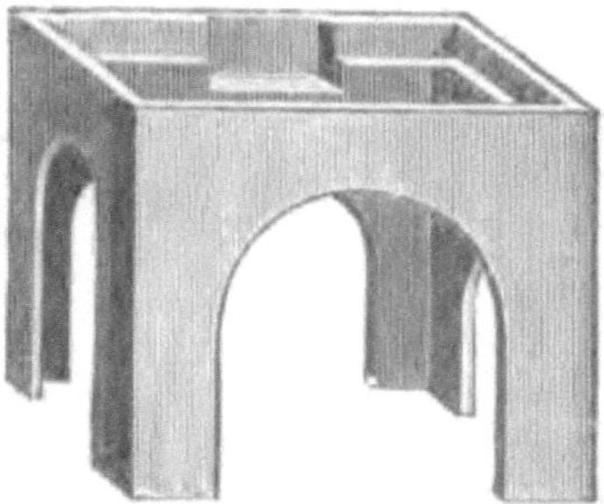

Fig. 63.—Swage Block Stand.

Punches are circular, square, oval, oblong, and wedge-shaped, and have handles of hazel or iron.　A punch, Fig. 71, and a bolster, Figs. 72 and 73, are often used together, the punch, by means of hammer blows, being driven through the red- or white-hot metal placed over the bolster.

Drifts are used to finish holes that have been

punched smaller than the finished dimensions, when
facilities for machining are not available.   They are
taper, as in Fig. 74, or parallel tools, having circular,

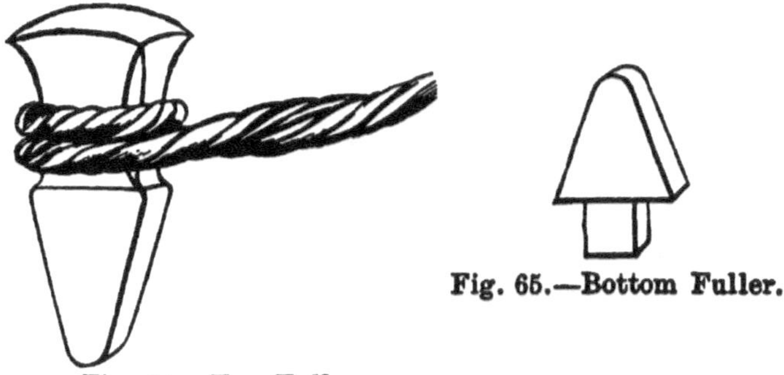

Fig. 64.—Top Fuller.

Fig. 65.—Bottom Fuller.

square, oblong, elliptical, or polygonal cross sections,
corresponding to those of the finished holes.   There is
scarcely a limit to the forms in which they may be

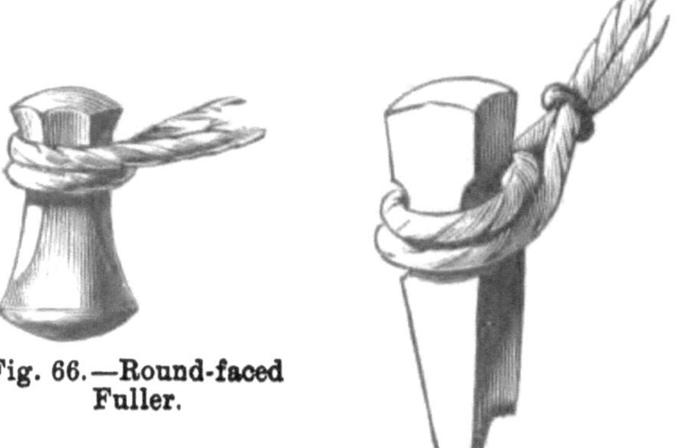

Fig. 66.—Round-faced
Fuller.

Fig. 67.—Hollow Fullering
Tool.

made and used.   Drifts are smooth, and, being driven
through the punched holes, enlarge, shape, and smooth
them while the metal is red-hot.   Two drifts are often
employed : one considerably tapering, so as to enlarge
the punched hole ; a second, the filler, or filling-in

piece, or mandrel, very slightly tapering, for imparting the precise finished dimensions.

Smooth drifts are rarely parallel; if they were, their withdrawal from a hole would be a matter of difficulty; the sides should taper not less than from two to four degrees.

The cutting drift partakes either of the nature of a

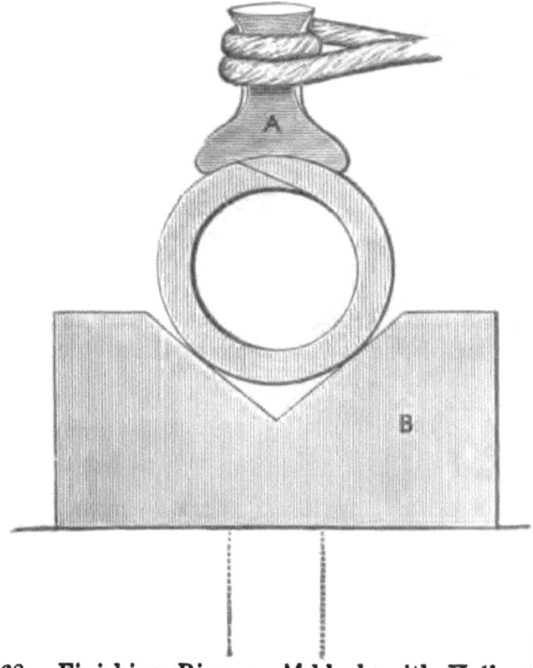

Fig. 68.—Finishing Ring on V-block with Hollow Tool.

sharp punch, or of a file. It does not open out the hole by pressure, and does not remove a large quantity of material at once; it merely smooths and finishes a hole already nearly to shape and size. Fig. 75 shows a drift for shallow holes, and Fig. 76 for deep ones; they are shaped with files from suitable blanks, and then tempered to a colour ranging from brown to purple. Toothed drifts for fine work have the teeth closer together; for coarse, rough work they are spaced farther apart. They are bevelled to allow clearance for the chips, being the equivalent of backing-

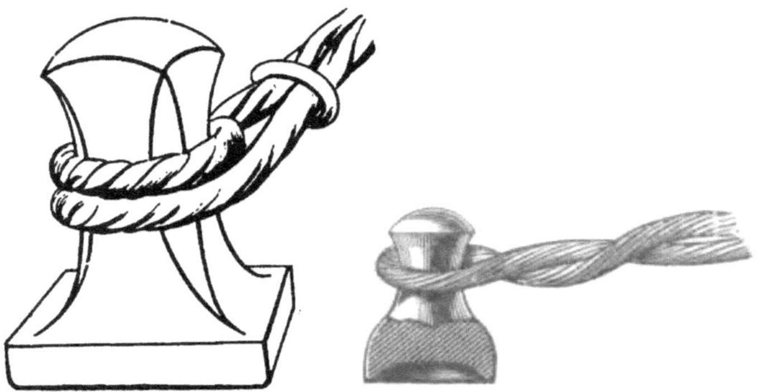

Fig. 69.—Flatter.   Fig. 70.—Cup Tool.

off in other cutting tools. For hard metal the angle between the cutting edge and the face is greater than for softer metals, thus following the usual practice in all

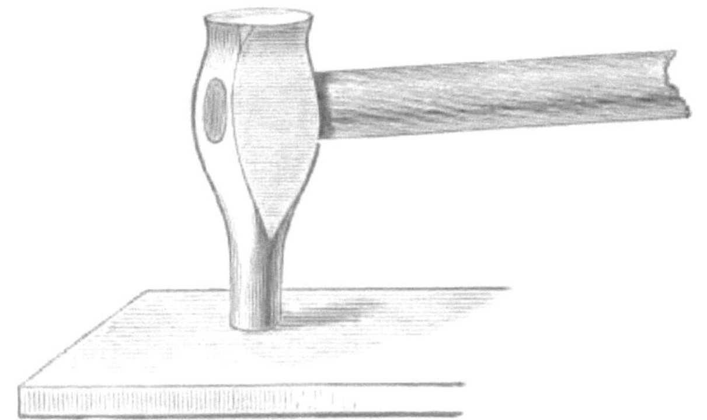

Fig. 71.—Round Punch on Thin Bar.

cutting tools. Oil should be supplied to the edges of the drift, and of the hole when driving it in, and the work should be bedded firmly on a block of metal; and care must be taken that the drift is driven straight. If the hole is deep, the drift must be withdrawn once or twice for clearance of chips. If the hole to be drifted is much smaller than the finished size, it will be necessary to enlarge it by chipping with a chisel.

Drifts with teeth are used for making round holes into square, oval, hexagonal, etc. It is better in these cases to work one-half the hole at a time. Thus, in

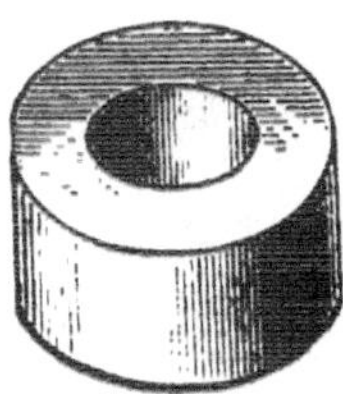

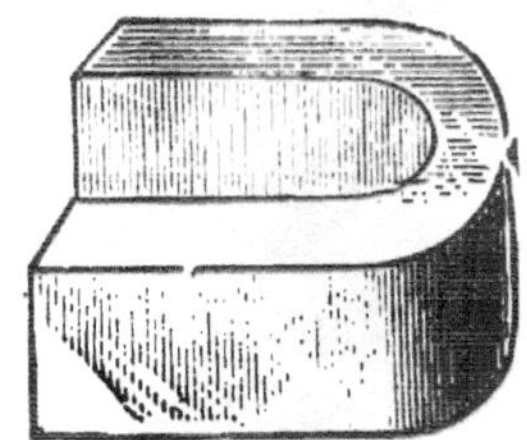

Fig. 72.   Bolsters.   Fig. 73.

drifting a round hole into a square one, one-half the round hole would be filled with a half-round plug, and a flat drift used to operate against the other half of the hole, little by little, thin backings being interposed one after the other. When one-half of the square is shaped, it is filled up, and the other half treated similarly. An elliptical hole is shaped in a similar way.

The drift is also serviceable for holes that do not

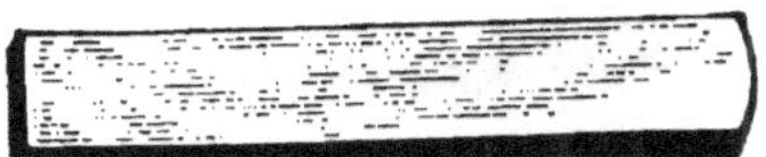

Fig. 74.—Tapered Drift.

pass quite through the material. As an example, for a rectangular hole to be smoothed in one direction, the drift shown in Fig. 77 could be used. The face, A, would remove a thin shaving. To take a second cut a thin strip of metal would be placed behind the drift; to take a third cut, an additional thin strip; and so on.

For drilling large holes, the ratchet-brace is a good tool. It can be fixed either upon a bench in a permanent position, or where wanted on work in hand. A press-drill thrust down with a lever is also a common appliance in country shops.   For a shop where much drilling is done, a double-geared hand or power drill is more efficient.

Dies are used by the smith when the initial cost of making them is likely to be repaid by the increased convenience and time saved.   They will be described later.

The heading tool, Fig. 78, is used for finishing the

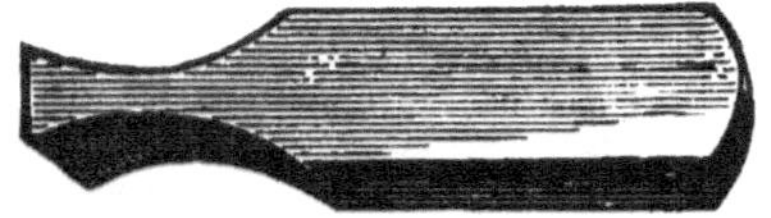

Fig. 75.—Drift for Shallow Holes.

shouldered ends formed on round bars.   The hole should be sufficiently large to take the bar whose end it is required to true.

Small tools—as tongs, swages, fullers, flatters, punches, and such like—accumulate in large numbers, and litter the place unless proper methods are employed to keep them in order.   Commonly, racks are fixed against the wall by the side of the forge.   These are

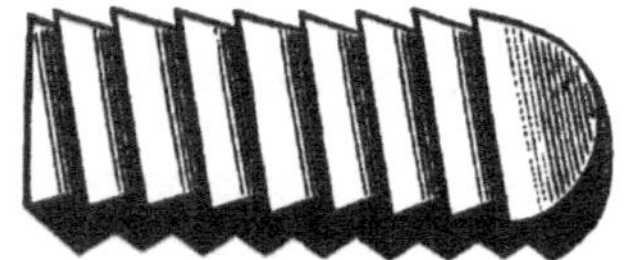

Fig. 76.—Drift for Deep Holes.

stout iron bars, supported parallel between uprights, at a distance of from 6 in. to 8 in. from the wall; the shanks or handles of the tools are dropped between these bars, their enlarged portions resting upon the top edges.   Tool racks are formed against the wall by driving two uprights into the ground at each end, and riveting the horizontal bars of iron to these.   The uprights and the bars are of flat iron—say, 2 in. by $\frac{1}{2}$ in.—placed edgewise.

For the lightest tools, handled with withies, or with round rods, it is sufficient to employ as racks short lengths of round rod riveted into flat bars. The flat bars are then secured to vertical uprights driven into the ground and leaning against the wall, and the rods stand out like spike nails. Upon these the light tools are hung by their handles. The flat bars may measure 2 in. by $\frac{1}{2}$ in., and the rods be of $\frac{1}{2}$-in. iron, 5 in. or 6 in. long. These lighter racks should be placed above the racks of parallel bars just previously described.

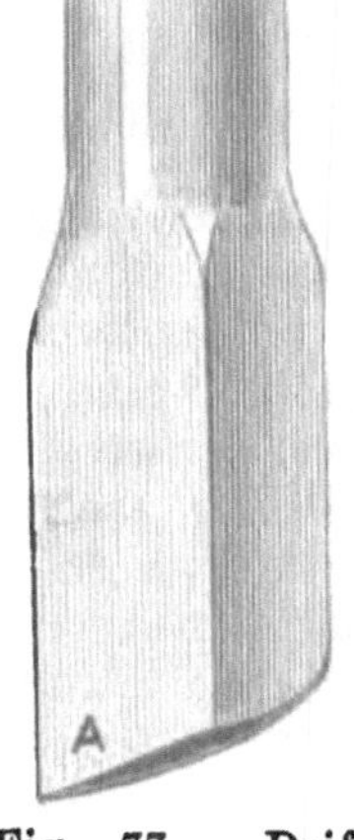

Fig. 77. — Drift used in Smoothing Holes.

Another method is to have an oblong open bench or stand of wood rigidly framed together. The top is crossed with bars or rods, leaving open spaces, in which the shanks or handles of the tools drop. Unless there is plenty of floor-room available, this is not so good as the rack, which occupies scarcely any floor-space.

For the heavier appliances used with the steam and other hammers, stands of a different kind are also used. Thus, two cast-iron standards of **A** form, with three or four pairs of internal brackets, carry between them stout deal

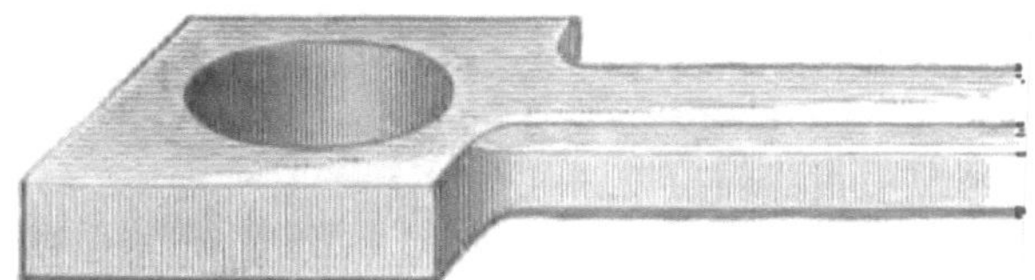

Fig. 78.—Heading Tool.

planks, which are bolted to the brackets. Upon these deals the heavy spring swages, die-blocks, etc., are laid side by side, the lighter on the top shelves, the heavier beneath, ready to hand.

D

CHAPTER III.

DRAWING DOWN AND UPSETTING.

BEFORE attempting to execute either of the processes of drawing down and upsetting dealt with in this chapter, it is necessary that the fire in which the iron is to be heated be properly made. The formation of the fire is of far greater importance than may be supposed.

The "stock" is the term given to the mass of hard-caked coal on a smith's hearth, within which the heat is confined ; and it also in some degree forms a reserve of fuel. But its primary purpose is to prevent radiation of the heat, and to cause its concentration upon the work in the hearth. If it were not for the stock, much of the heat would go up the chimney, and the work also would be oxidised more rapidly than it is, by reason of its partial exposure to the air. The size and shape of the stock evidently depend on those of the work. The stock consists of two portions—one lying against the tuyere and hearth-back, the other placed opposite to the first in the direction of the coal and water bunks, the work lying midway between the two. The only portion of the fire that is replenished to any considerable degree, in the course of a day's work, is that central portion. The stock, though highly heated, does not burn away sensibly, because it is protected from the direct action of the blast, and the upper portions are kept damp. Yet the inner faces, being in direct contact with fuel supplied from time to time to the central part of the fire, are at a glow with heat.

To make a fire, therefore, the stock is first built at the back and front of the hearth, and beaten hard with the slice or with the sledge, the choking of the tuyere hole being prevented by passing an iron rod temporarily into it. The fire is then lit in the central portions with a handful of shavings and a little coal, assisted by a gentle blast.

Forgings of unequal sectional area are formed either by drawing down, upsetting, or welding, or by a combination of the three processes. Generally, the choice between these three methods is not made because one is essentially superior to the other regarded simply as a question of ultimate result , but because under given circumstances it either involves less work, or economises material, or is the only way possible with material that happens to be in stock, or because there are odds and ends that it is desirable to use up ; or, lastly, because it is the best method available with the

Fig. 79.—Square Bar Drawn Down.

tools and help at the disposal of the smith. The alternative, therefore, is commonly one of expediency.

It is often, however, a question of relative dimensions. If the difference between the enlarged and the reduced part is very great, neither drawing down nor upsetting would be resorted to, unless for some exceptional reason, but welding would be employed. The same holds good in other forging ; as, for example, in the case of eyes. An eye having a small hole and much metal around it, as that of the tie-rod of an iron roof truss, would have that end forged solid, and the hole punched through. But an eye, having a large hole and relatively little metal around it, and so possessing more the character of a loop, would be bent round and welded. An eye of medium thickness may obviously be made in either fashion.

To draw down a piece of iron proceed as follows :— Suppose the portion marked A, Fig. 79, has to be drawn down from a bar originally of the size of B. The bar

is laid across the edge of the anvil in a slightly inclined
direction, and nicked at c, Fig. 80, with a top fuller.
If both sides of the bar have to be drawn down, then a
bottom fuller would be inserted in the anvil in opposition to the top fuller, and the bar would be nicked as in
Fig. 81. Chisels or sets are not used in such nicking,
for these would divide the fibres of the metal, while the
round-faced fullers simply alter their direction without
breaking their continuity.

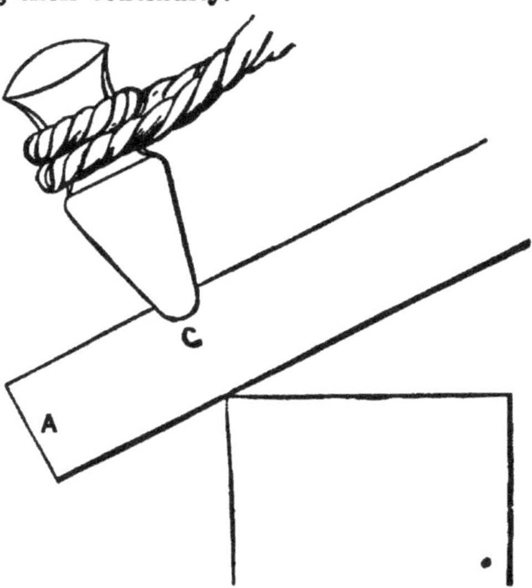

Fig. 80.—Nicking with Top Fuller.

The preservation of the continuity of the fibre is of
primary importance in forged work, so that what may
appear to be roundabout methods which give much
extra trouble will often be resorted to in order to
preserve that continuity. Fibre or "grain" should
never be severed. Few of the tools used by the smith
for shaping to outline have absolutely square edges ; they
are all more or less rounding. Thus the continuity of
the fibre is preserved, however it is bent and twisted.
A bar of iron held in the vice and bent until it is
doubled shows on the outside radius the torn ends,

which look like bundles of vegetable fibre, and not unlike torn animal muscle. A specimen torn asunder in a testing machine has its fibrous structure still more apparent, though not so clearly as in the bending process, in which the outer skin will present a most characteristic striation or shrivelling in the longitudinal direction.

Fibrous iron may readily be changed into a weak crystalline material by nicking with a sharp tool, or by excessive hammering. A bar of iron, nicked round, and broken off suddenly, shows fractured surfaces as highly crystalline as those of cast iron. This clearly proves the necessity of making fullers, and other shaping or moulding tools, with edges rounding.

When the work has been nicked with the fuller, the metal along A (Figs. 79 and 81) is drawn down or

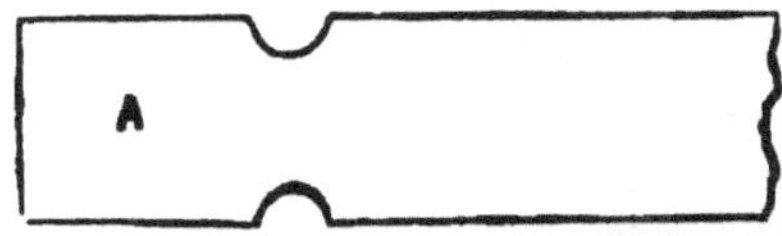

Fig. 81.—Bar nicked with Top and Bottom Fullers.

thinned by a succession of blows from the hand hammer or sledge, with or without previous fullering. When fullering tools are used, the top fuller would be employed singly if only the one face requires reduction, or in pairs, one above the other, if both faces have to be drawn down. The effect is that a succession of depressions are formed upon the surface of the spread-out work with ridges between, and these have to be obliterated with the hammer.

Fullering and hammering not only lengthen the bar, but also spread it sideways. If the bar is to be equal-sided, the widening has to be prevented by rapidly hammering the sides alternately with the faces. After every few blows are given on the faces, the smith turns the bar quarter round during the brief interval between a couple of blows, and the iron receives several blows upon the edges as a corrective to those on the faces, and its equal sidedness is thus preserved during the process of drawing down. By practice, this rapid changing of the faces on the anvil is accomplished without damaging the rectangular form.

In drawing down, whether with fullering tools, or with the hammer alone, as is frequently done where the reduction in area does not amount to much, the process of thinning always commences at the end of the iron farthest from the smith, and proceeds towards himself. One inch and a half or two inches is drawn down at a time, and the work is thus rendered easier than if a larger surface were taken at once.

When the iron is first roughed down, its surface will not be smooth, though a good smith can impart a very fair finish to a flat surface by the hammer alone. The hammers should strike so as to bruise the work as little as possible. There is a knack in using the hammer so that its edges will not mark the work, the blow being given by the central rounding portion of the face only. Striking fair with the middle of the hammer face, each mark serves to partly obliterate others, and leaves a very smooth surface, only slightly wavy. This is all that a smith working single-handed can effect by way of finish. With the assistance of a hammerman the surface can be smoothed more effectually by means of a flatter, which is held with the right hand of the smith, and slid in turn all over the surface of the work while the hammerman strikes it with the sledge. Thus finished, the work is left very smooth.

In drawing down a round bar the process is the same in principle, but slightly different in detail. The rod will be nicked round with a fuller and drawn down under the hammer, beginning as before at the end farthest from the hand. A fullering tool is not used for extending the metal, which is done with the hammer only, and the rod is rotated between each hammer blow. Toward the close of the operation, smoothness is imparted by means of swages, the work lying in a bottom swage of nearly semicircular form, see Fig. 82, which shows an anvil swage fitted into the hole in the anvil, while blows are struck upon the rod's upper surface with a hand hammer, if the smith be single-handed, or, if the smith has a striker, with the sledge upon a top swage the counterpart in form of the bottom. In Fig. 82 A indicates the top and B the bottom swages, with the bar of iron, C, between them; D is the anvil.

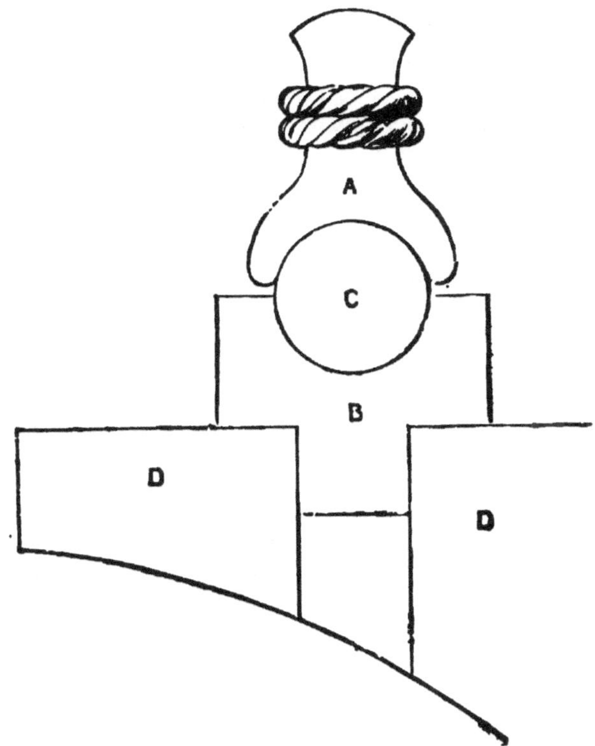

Fig. 82.—Round Bar between Top and Bottom Swages.

By means of suitable spring swages, previously described, a smith, working single-handed, can sometimes make use of the top as well as of the bottom tool.

With a steam hammer this work of drawing down and finishing is very much simplified. It is then not even necessary to use top or bottom fullers, for, having marked the position of the shoulders on the bar, the smith lays the bar on the anvil of the steam hammer, and draws down the work directly between it and the tup or hammer, turning the bar quickly during each period of ascent of the tup. If the bar is of large size and of considerable length, the drawing down will still have to be done in short lengths, two or three inches from the end being drawn down first, and the bar being then thrust farther along, and the succeeding portions drawn down. The bar is always held perfectly flat, and the hammer finishes at once.

For rod work, top and bottom swages of the spring type are placed under the tup at the finishing stage. The rod is first drawn down roughly between the anvil and the tup, being rotated rapidly between each blow, a rudely circular form being imparted or preserved simultaneously with the process of drawing down Before the reduction is quite complete, the spring swages are placed on the anvil, held by an attendant, the work inserted between them, and rounded and finished by a few final blows of the tup on the top swage—the work still being revolved during each period of ascent of the tup.

While these processes are being carried out, and with the iron at a red heat, a scale of oxide forms rapidly. The larger the forging, the greater the quantity of the oxide formed. This should be brushed away with a switch of brushwood as fast as it forms, otherwise it will be driven by the hammer blows into the surface of the work, and form a rough scale, which is afterwards both unsightly and a hindrance to easy tooling in the vice or lathe. Where the forgings are large, a man stands by the steam hammer and brushes away the scale after every half-dozen or so blows. At the anvil the striker or the smith knocks the scale off immediately the iron is removed from the fire, and afterwards as often as it may be required.

To judge the length of iron to be allowed for drawing down is not difficult to a practised smith. Few trouble to calculate in figures the length required.

Yet, when working the best and most expensive qualities of iron and steel, it is as well to bear in mind a rule of simple proportion. The original section of a bar bears the same proportion to a given reduced section that the length of the latter bears to that of the former. Thus if a bar originally 3 in. square has to be reduced to an inch square, one inch in length of the 3 in. bar will be taken for reduction to a 3 in. length of one inch square. If the reduced portion is tapered, or of unequal and varying dimensions, then the mean of the various sectional areas must be taken. Additional allowance must be made for ragged and perhaps burnt ends, and a trifle for inaccuracy in cutting off.

The time different smiths will be occupied over a given piece of work differs greatly. A smart smith will always do as much work as possible upon a forging in a single heat. While his iron is in the fire, he will mentally go through the sequence of operations, and see that whatever is required is at hand, and when the iron is on the anvil he will strike quickly while the iron is hot. In some examples to be given, the number of heats in which work ought to be forged will be stated approximately.

Upsetting, or jumping up, is one of the alternatives of drawing down. By this method the metal is knocked or jumped up into a mass larger in area than the bar itself. Upsetting is a slower and more laborious process than drawing down. A smart smith will draw down several inches of bar at one heat ; but to upset a very moderate mass of metal will require several heats. Hence it is not possible to treat in this way any very large-shouldered portion ; in this case the plan is to weld on a ring or collar, or a solid mass of metal, according to circumstances. Except the iron be cut off sufficiently short to go endwise under the hammer, the use of this tool is not possible in upsetting. However, the monkey, or swinging pendulum hammer, fulfils the purpose of the hand hammer.

The method of upsetting to form a collar, A (Fig. 83),

upon the end of a rod whose original section is that of
B, and without welding the collar on as a ring, is as
follows :—The end which is to form A is enclosed in the
fire, but no more of that end is heated than the precise

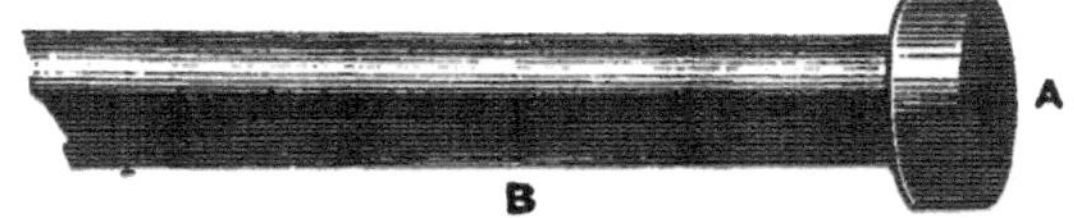

Fig. 83.—Bar with Collar on End.

amount required to be upset; that portion of the rod
which joins it is kept quite cool and black by heaping
damp coal around it.   The end is then brought nearly
or quite to a welding heat, and taken from the fire.

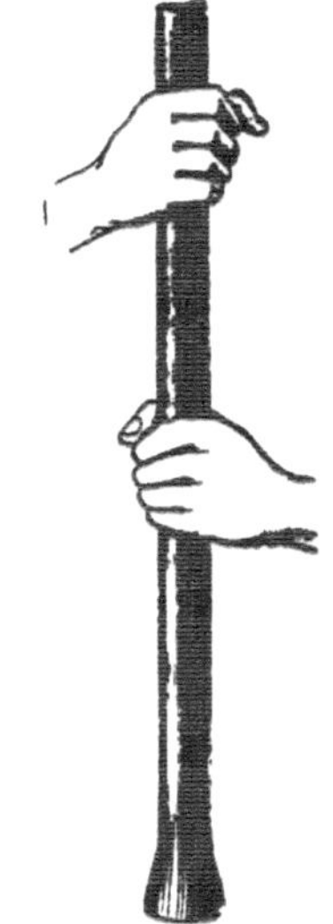

Fig. 84.—Jumping
Bar Vertically.

Sometimes on removal from the
fire, and just before upsetting, the
extreme face of the heated end is
dipped into the water trough to
chill it, and so the better to prepare it to resist the blows of the
hammer; but this is not always
done.

The actual upsetting is performed in one of several ways.
The bar may be held in both hands
(Fig. 84) in a vertical position, and
the white-hot end jumped down
repeatedly upon the anvil face,
or upon the plate of cast-iron
which is often let into the ground
alongside of the anvil stand for
this purpose.   Another way is to
lay the bar in a horizontal position
upon the anvil face (Fig. 85),
holding it in one hand if light, and with a hand
hammer, hammering the end to be upset.   Or, if it
is heavy, it may be held in both hands, or, perhaps,
slung in a chain from the forge crane, and upset with a
sledge hammer.   When very heavy, it is laid upon the

anvil face or upon a levelling block, and the swinging monkey is driven against it.

Three or four heats are often required to jump up a moderate mass of metal. The result is, that fairly exact dimensions are not at once obtainable by this method, as in the case of drawing down. The jumped-up mass of metal, in spite of much care in localising the heat precisely where it is required, is very unequal, and quite without sharp shoulders. Hence, considerably more metal has to be massed together than is actually required in the completed wo:k. in order to allow of

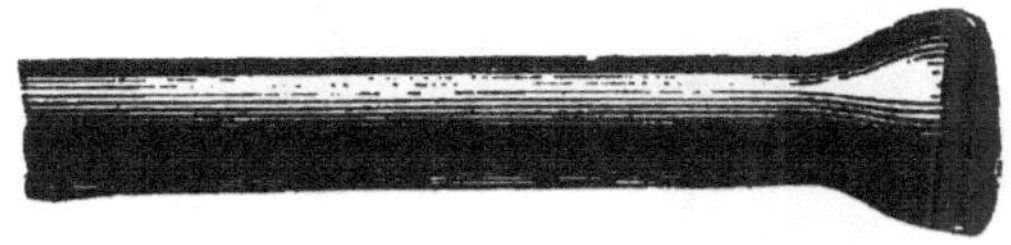

Fig. 85.—Upsetting Bar Horizontally.

symmetrical finish to size. Upsetting tends to separate the fibres of the metal. It is, therefore, necessary to counteract this by hammering the jumped up portion at a welding heat. When the metal for the collar is massed in sufficient quantity, it is finished parallel in swages, and the square shoulder finished with a set hammer or flatter, or in swages, and the end with hammer and flatter.

A collar can be also formed upon any portion of a bar situated away from the ends by localising the heat in the position required, and then jumping up the metal at that particular place, until sufficient mass is obtained for finishing to size and shape. Any other sections can be heated, and the spreading out can be performed by upsetting in one direction more than in others.

CHAPTER IV.

WELDING AND PUNCHING.

WELDABILITY is one of the most valuable properties possessed by wrought iron and mild steel. Welding is often the alternative of drawing down or of upsetting; correct heat and cleanliness are the chief requisites. Welding heat corresponds with that temperature at which the metal is in a state of partial fusion on the surface. At that temperature it is extremely plastic,

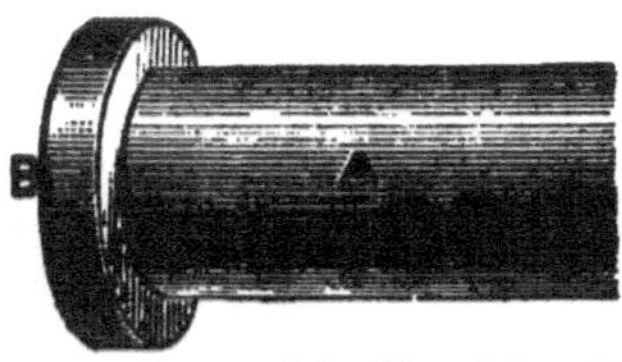

Fig. 86.—Bar with Shouldered End.

and a little hammering will cause two surfaces to adhere and possess as much strength as the other parts of the metal. The welding heats for iron and steel differ, and even also the heats for different qualities of iron and different qualities of steel. Any iron will require a much greater heat than steel, and the better the quality of the iron, the higher the welding heat that it will stand without becoming burned. At a welding heat iron gives off dazzling sparks; steel shows only an intense yellow, and gives off few sparks. The ascertaining of the correct heat is a matter for experience entirely, and no description or illustration can take the place of practical lessons.

To illustrate the process of welding more clearly, two plain examples, one a collared rod, and the other a plain straight rod, are given.

Taking the shouldered end (Fig. 86), first cut off the rod, A, and then prepare to fit over it the ring, B, for which take a square bar, say ⅛ in. larger than the finished section required, and, with a hot set, cut off

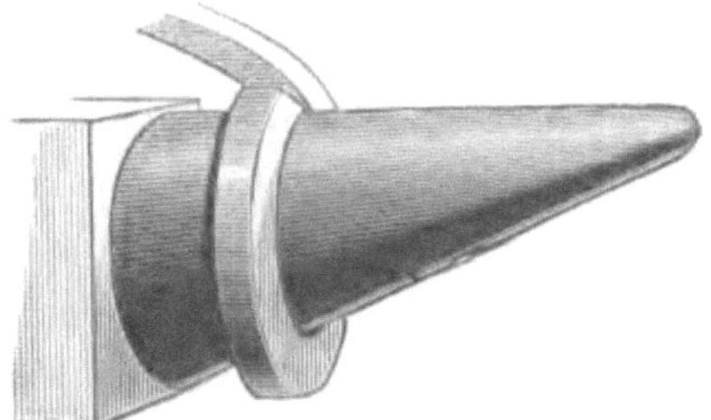

Fig. 87.—Forming Ring on Anvil Beak.

one end diagonally or else fuller it down. Then bend the bar roughly into circular form over the anvil horn (Fig. 87), and cut off to the required length, with a sloping face to lap upon and match the first diagonal. The metal must have sufficient lap to allow for welding

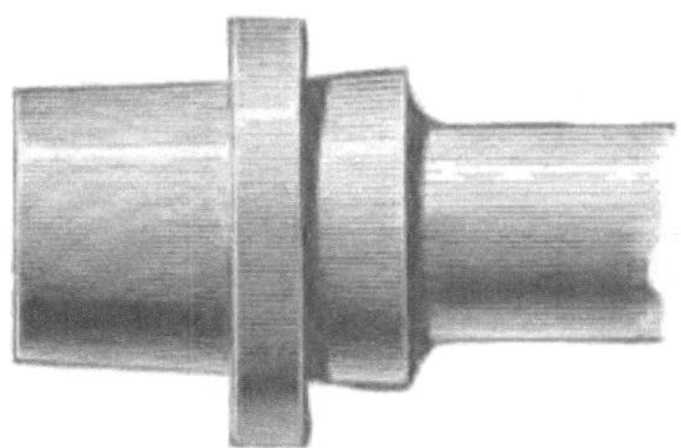

Fig. 88.—Ring slipped over Mandril.

and for dressing off and finishing. If the ring is fairly true, it will be ready to go into the fire for welding; but if not, slip it over a mandrel, Fig. 88, and give the scarfed joint a neat appearance, either with the hammer alone or with one of the hollow tools previously described. Then slip off the ring and flatten the faces (Fig. 89). This is precisely the plan that would be adopted in welding a separate ring.

To weld it to the rod, the ring is slipped over the end of the rod, care being taken to remove any scale adherent to either, and they are then put into the clear fire. Sand may be sprinkled over the work, but with a clear fire it is not necessary, and is frequently not done. When the welding heat is attained, which for

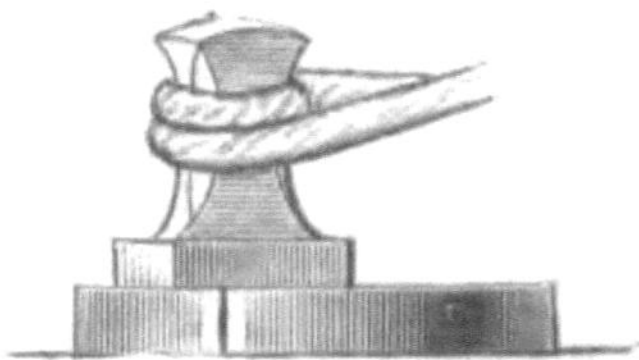

Fig. 89.—Smoothing Faces of Ring with Flatter.

wrought iron is of a dazzling whiteness, when the iron seems ready to melt, and particles appear ready to drop off, and a rapid evolution of sparks takes place, the work is removed from the fire, placed on a **V**-block (B, Fig. 68, p. 45), and the scarf joint and the ring are hammered all round with a hand hammer, the rod with its ring being continually turned into fresh positions on the **V**-block.

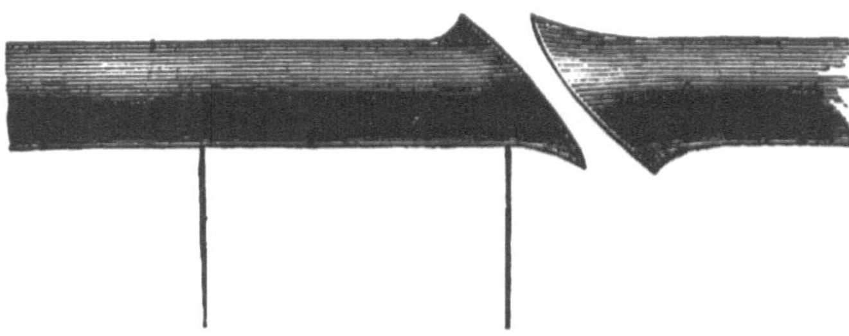

Fig. 90.—Ends Scarfed and Upset ready for Welding.

If a hammerman's services are available, the hollow tool is used, and a few blows upon it consolidate and smooths the surfaces. Then the faces and shoulders are finished by means of a heading tool, having a hole of a size suitable to take the rod, a few blows with hammer and flatter finishing off both the under shouldered face and the upper flat face. Then it may be necessary to work over the circular part again with the hollow tool. This is to finish the surface, for the welding heat is soon past, and if the union of the joint faces is not fully effected in the first few seconds it will be more or less imperfect.

To weld a rod a scarfed joint is employed, and plenty of metal is wanted to allow for hammering the joint together and for finishing it afterwards without reducing below correct sizes; therefore, the ends of the bar have not only to be scarfed, but to be slightly upset. The meeting ends, which have been cut off square, are laid horizontally upon the anvil, and are upset or beaten over, while nearly at a welding heat. Then they are laid over the edge of the anvil, and scarfed or beaten down diagonally with a fullering tool, the face of the scarf being made rounding rather than hollow. Both ends having been served precisely alike, they are put back into the fire, and raised to the welding heat. Lift the work vertically out from the fire; do not drag it through the coal. Any particles of dirt that are present will show as dark specks on the white-hot iron, and should be brushed off with a switch of brushwood.

The smith and his helper lay the scarfed ends together, as shown in Fig. 90, and then two or three blows with the hand hammer cause the ends to unite, and the rod can then be rapidly turned about on the anvil while the joint is consolidated all round with hand hammers or sledges. The top and bottom swages can be used for imparting the finish required. It will be apparent that without the first enlargement or upsetting of the rods, the process of welding and swaging would have thinned the rod at the welded section below that of the other portions. How much to upset and how much to scarf are matters for experience.

These notes on welding are somewhat of an elementary character, but further information on the subject will be embodied in the descriptions of working miscellaneous examples.

Punching, drifting, and drilling are the three methods by which the smith commonly makes holes in metal. The first two are performed on red-hot iron and steel; the last, and sometimes the second also, on cold metal. Drifts, and the method of using them, are dealt with in the chapter on hand tools (see pp. 43 to 47), and at present punching alone will be treated upon.

Punches may be used to make a clean, finished hole, to which nothing is done subsequently, and which is quite good enough for its purpose. In other cases, punching, like the coring of castings, takes out the bulk of the metal, leaving a certain small allowance for finishing with drill, reamer or boring tool.

Generally the details of the process of punching are as follows:—The iron to be punched, being brought to a suitable heat, full red or white, is laid across the anvil, and the punch is driven by means of blows from a sledge or hand hammer, about half-way through. The punch is then withdrawn, and the iron is turned over and laid upon its opposite face. A dark spot indicates where the chilling effect of the punch has taken place, and enables the smith to set the punch again in position for piercing the metal so that the holes meet. During the formation of the second portion, the work is either laid upon a bolster or over the hole in the anvil, and the punch then passes freely through.

If the hole is deep, the hot iron closes and tightens around the punch, and the latter is therefore withdrawn at every three or four blows. Further, the heat of the iron makes the punch very hot, so that after every three or six blows it is necessary to cool the punch in water.

Methods of producing punched holes vary according to circumstances. If it is desired to preserve the same amount of metal all around, the hole is partly punched and partly drifted or opened out. Obviously, when a hole is punched entirely with a flat-ended tool like Fig. 71, p. 46, the metal removed is equal in area to the area of the point of the punch itself, and the width of the bar is only very slightly perceptibly increased (see Fig. 91).

Another way of making a hole without weakening the bar to any great extent, is by means of a conical punch, which may be inserted, and the hole formed and

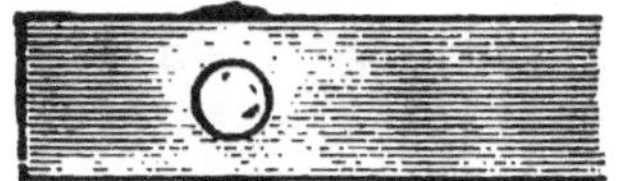

Fig. 91.—Material removed by Flat-ended Punch.

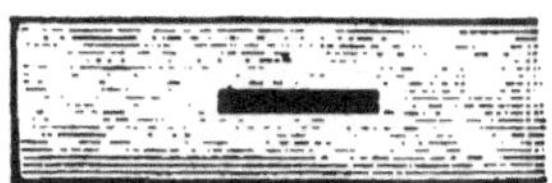

Fig. 92.—Commencing Hole with Hot Set.

opened, without the removal of any appreciable quantity of material. Or if a hot set is driven from one side half-way through the bar, and half-way from the other (Fig. 92), a punch or drift can be driven in afterwards,

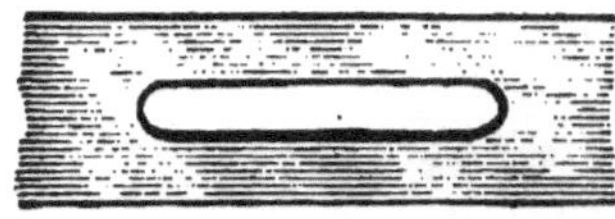

Fig. 93.—Slotted Hole ; Area Reduced.

and the slit opened out into circular or oblong form, as may be required.

Long slot-holes are cut in two ways. In one, holes are punched at each end of the intended slot equal to its width, and the metal between is cut out with the hot

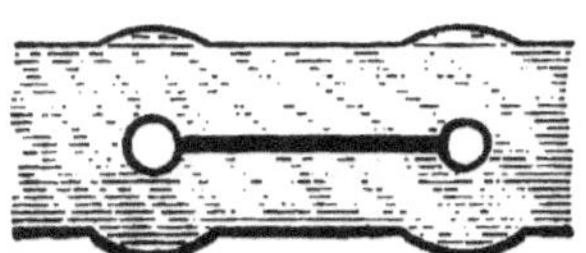

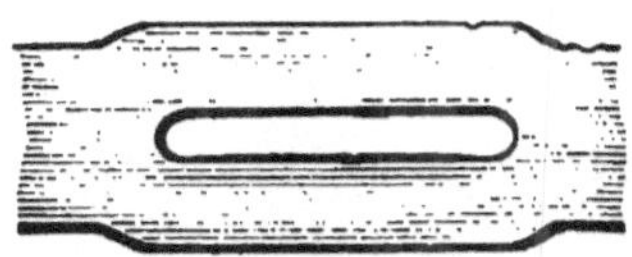

Figs. 94 and 95.—Slotted Holes ; Area Retained

set, cutting from opposite sides in succession, and meeting in the middle (Fig. 93). In the other, holes are punched at each end, and a chisel cut made centrally from hole to hole, and a drift inserted and the metal opened out (Figs. 94 and 95). In this way the flanking metal is thrust out sideways, and the bulk of its section

E

retained. Such a slot-hole is finished by inserting a drift or mandrel of the correct section, and hammering the outside edges of the bar upon it.

When punching holes, it is necessary to take account of the direction of the fibre. Unless attention is given to this, the iron will become divided instead of spread out. Punching puts considerable tension on the fibres around the hole. with reduction of area, and it is

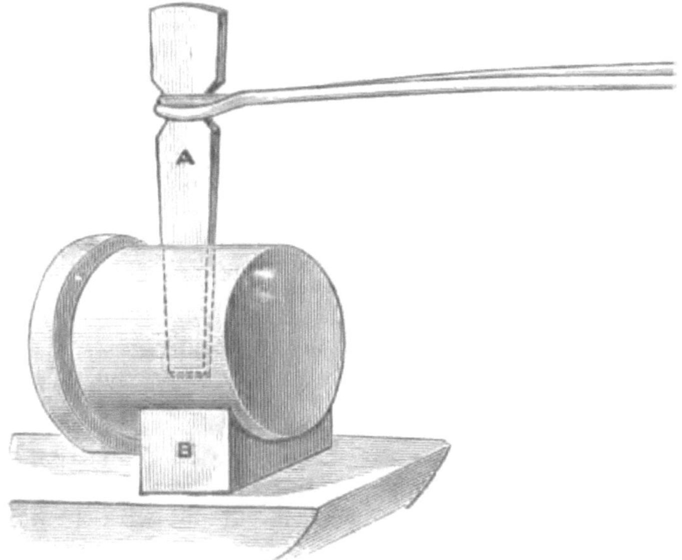

Fig. 96.—Punching a Hole through a Stout Pin.

an operation, therefore, that requires to be done with judgment.

To punch slotted cottar ways in which the section of the iron is not enlarged, take a tapered oblong punch or drift of steel, like that shown at A, Fig. 96, with rounding ends. Raise the iron to a welding heat, and properly support it according to its shape, upon a bolster or a bottom tool, and drive the punch half-way into it. Turn the iron over, cool the punch in water, and drive it in exactly opposite to the first position, until the openings meet at the centre of the bar. The slightly-tapered punch makes a hole doubly tapered, which is also rough. A parallel drift or filling-piece is then driven into the hole, which accommodates itself to the form of the filling-piece. The outside of the iron is smoothed and finished, and when the shape is completed the filling-piece is driven out. This method of finishing a job while a central punch, drift, filling-in piece, or mandrel remains in the work, is adopted in many classes of work.

Punching a hole through a stout pin is illustrated by Fig. 96, the pin selected being $3\frac{1}{4}$ in. diameter; the hole measures $1\frac{1}{4}$ in. by $\frac{1}{2}$ in., and is made at one heat. The punch, as shown, has its body below the handle, about 6 in. long, and is tapered. The pin being brought to a white heat, the punch is driven almost through. Then the pin is turned over and the punch driven into the darker spot which has appeared, and the hole is thus completed. During the punching the tool has to be several times cooled in water. At the first stage of making the hole, the pin lies upon an ordinary bottom swage. At the second stage it lies upon a bolster, B, in form like a hollow swage, but pierced with a central hole, through which the drift can find a clear way.

As the hole is thus roughly punched, the metal around it will be partly compressed, partly bulged ; very little is actually driven out and removed by the punch. The bulging of the pin is corrected by hammering between top and bottom swages, and then the hole is finished by drifting, all being done during the one heat. During the punching, whenever the punch is withdrawn to be cooled, a little small coal is strewn in the punched hole, to burn up the gas which would otherwise resist the passage of the punch.

CHAPTER V.

CONDITIONS OF WORK ; PRINCIPLES OF FORMATION.

THE smith works under three conditions, each of which ought to receive separate treatment. These are:—first, when he works alone, without the assistance of a striker, or of steam power, or of dies; second, when he has the assistance of a striker or hammer-man, but is still without steam power; third, when he has the help of a hammer-man, and has also the use of a steam hammer, and dies of various kinds. Amateurs and many country and jobbing smiths come under the first category. Men in small workshops come under the second; whilst the third class embraces the men in large engineering and general iron works.

It is obvious that the particular circumstances under which work has to be performed must often modify the methods adopted. For example, a smith who has the use of a steam hammer will either swage or draw down, when such is practicable, in preference to upsetting and welding. Again, a smith who has command of dies and steam hammer will not spend so much time in finishing and smoothing the surfaces, angles, and corners of his work upon the anvil, because he can put his roughed work between a pair of dies, and finish it with a few blows of the steam hammer. The smith who has no help from a striker will be restricted to the very lightest work. Iron of nearly the finished sizes and sections wanted will have to be used. Extensive drawing down and welding cannot be done; little is possible beyond work that can be done with the hand hammer. Swages, flatters, fullers, and chisels—except the anvil cutters— are of scarcely any use when there is available only one pair of hands for holding the work and the tools.

The class of work that comes within the range of the unassisted smith differs from that of the worker who is favoured in the matter of assistance and tools. But he has still all the wealth of ornamental work, like that done by mediæval smiths, all tool work—almost anything, in fact, where the sections of iron and steel do not exceed, say, 1 in. to 1¼ in. in diameter. Obviously, the choice of forges, tools, as well as methods of work, will be different under these several conditions.

In the judicious choice of that which is the best out of several possible methods, lies much of the skill of the experienced smith. It by no means follows that a method by which a piece of work can be forged to shape is necessarily the quickest, cheapest, or best; or that which may be the best method under certain conditions is the best in all or any circumstances. One often has to adopt a method which may not be best from another's point of view, because he either does not possess the iron of proper sections, or the special tools, or other necessary assistance. This fact is made more forcible when the numerous sections of iron required by the all-round smith are considered. Even in large shops where steam hammers are available, it is often impossible to manipulate the heavier sections of iron. These require very powerful hammers, in order that the force of their blows shall penetrate to the interior of the mass. Hence many engineers find it necessary to order for massive work specially heavy forgings, or "uses" as they are called at the rolling mills.

The material of a single-handed smith, and that of an amateur, is limited to small sections. With a small forge no great heat is possible, and a smith working single-handed cannot manipulate any heavy sections. Bars of iron are made in lengths of several feet, and the purchasing of a fair stock of entire bars of several sizes would prove a heavy expense. It is best to select a few bars of the most useful dimensions, according to the class of work which it is intended chiefly to do, and when any other sections happen to be wanted, to purchase them in short lengths from a local smith or at an iron stores.

The principal shapes of iron used by the smith are "round," "square," and "flat" bars. These are made in almost all ordinary dimensions, and in different qualities. The published lists of sections rolled at some of the best known iron and steel works in this country are here made use of.

The bars are rolled in the following Wire Gauge sizes, 7, 6, 5, 4, 3, 2, 1; and also ranging from $\frac{3}{16}$ in. up to $2\frac{3}{8}$ in., increasing by sixteenths; from $2\frac{3}{8}$ in. to 5 in., increasing by eighths; from 5 in. to $5\frac{1}{4}$ in. by quarters; from $5\frac{1}{4}$ in. to 6 in. by eighths; and from 6 in. to $6\frac{1}{2}$ in. by quarters; and each of these can be rolled to "full," and "bare," as well as to exact sizes. Thus there are obtainable sixty-eight different diameters of round bar, from $\frac{3}{16}$ in. to $6\frac{1}{2}$ in.

The squares increase from $\frac{3}{16}$ in. to $1\frac{3}{8}$ in. by sixteenths; from $1\frac{3}{8}$ in. to 4 in. by eighths; from 4 in. to $5\frac{1}{2}$ in. by quarters; and from $5\frac{1}{4}$ in. to $6\frac{1}{4}$ in. by half-inches; giving fifty-one sizes in square sections from $\frac{3}{16}$ in. to $6\frac{1}{2}$. in.

The flats range from $\frac{3}{8}$ in. to 12 in. wide, in almost all thicknesses from $\frac{1}{4}$ in. upwards, advancing by sixteenths and eighths. Flats in sixty-five different widths are obtainable.

This iron is made in four qualities—the "ordinary," or common, "best," "best, best," and "best, best, best."

Good metal being rather costly, a careful smith will preserve odds and ends of iron and steel for small work, and for welding to other portions, so saving the cutting off of small pieces from long bars.

It is not economical to buy inferior iron. The quantities used in light work are so small that the saving is scarcely worth taking account of, while inferior iron is a constant source of anxiety to the smith.

The differences in the qualities of iron are broadly

these. A good iron is silvery and clean-looking ; a bad iron is dull and dirty by comparison. A good iron is free or nearly free from flaws, which in a bad iron always show up when it is brought to a red heat. They are due to the intermixed cinder and scale left by insufficient puddling. The way to get rid of some of these is to subject the iron to a welding heat, and hammer it thoroughly all over to consolidate it in some degree.

Carbon, manganese, phosphorus, and silicon exercise so vital an influence upon the numerous alloys of iron and copper as in many cases to totally and absolutely change its appearance and physical qualities. But in wrought iron, where the foreign ingredients seldom amount to more than 1 per cent., being often only ½ per cent., those very minute admixtures are found to affect the metal to an extent that makes itself very evident at the anvil. The most readily forged, whether hot or cold, is that which is the purest. Iron that will forge well while hot, but not when cold, is said to be "cold short," and this is due to very minute quantities of phosphorus, antimony, and silicon. When iron is apt to develop cracks while being forged hot, it is said to be "hot short," and this may be due to a minute quantity of sulphur, whose amount may not perhaps exceed ·03 per cent., or it may be due to antimony. Only delicate chemical analysis could demonstrate the presence of these foreign elements, but the smith sees their results when the iron is under the hammer and punch.

The most striking characteristic of wrought iron that has been rolled is its fibrous condition, and this occurs also, in a lesser degree, in mild steel. This is the quality by which it can be shaped according to the will of the smith. It is a remarkable property of these fibrous materials that the very qualification that is of so much value can be changed or modified in the working. A bar of iron placed across the anvil cutter and nicked around with a chisel, may be broken short off with little effort, and a practised eye is necessary to detect whether the iron is cast or wrought by the appearance of the fracture, which is wholly crystalline. The same bar bent without nicking, or gradually torn asunder until it breaks, shows the fracture wholly fibrous, the long, string-like fibres becoming drawn out as though the bar had been built up of innumerable fine strings of metal. Again, if a crank-shaft or a lever-arm breaks at a sharp re-entrant angle, the fracture will be crystalline. But if it breaks at an angle whose faces are gradually merged into one another with a curve or hollow, the fracture will be fibrous.

It follows from the fibrous character of wrought iron

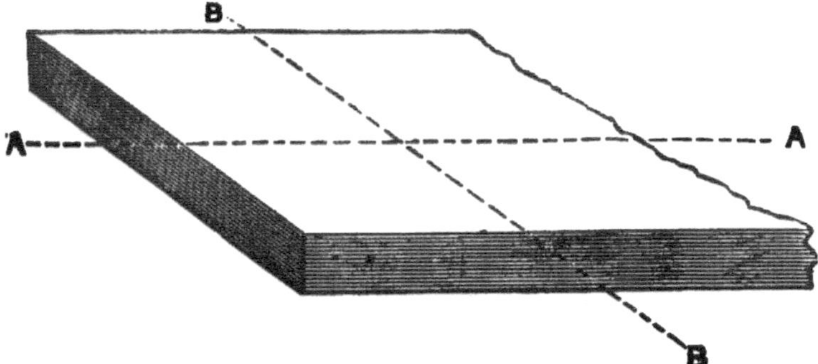

Fig. 97.—Direction of Fibre in Iron Bar.

developed during rolling, that it must be considerably stronger in the direction in which it is rolled (A, A, Fig. 97) than in the transverse direction, B, B. The difference is in about the ratio of 21 to 17—that is, if it would require 21 tons per inch to break the bar through the line B, B, in a direction at right angles with A, A—that is, across the fibres—17 tons would suffice to break it along A, A—that is, along or with the fibres. This holds good to a very slight extent only in mild steel, where the rolling is only incidental to the shaping. The direction and relative strength of fibre have a most marked influence upon design in wrought iron. It shows why the direction in which work is subjected to the greater stress, should always coincide with the longitudinal direction of the fibres ; why curved work should not be cut from the solid, thereby severing the continuity of the grain, if it is possible to bend it round and so preserve the fibres continuous. It shows why in many cases it is better to split or divide a bar, and bend or fork it, so preserving continuity of grain, rather than to slot out or to weld on. It explains many practical points in the working of wrought iron as distinguished from the working of the homogeneous mild steels. It shows the advantage of keeping the edges rounding and not sharp on fullering and similar tools, by whose use the grain is not violently severed, but rather bent to shape.

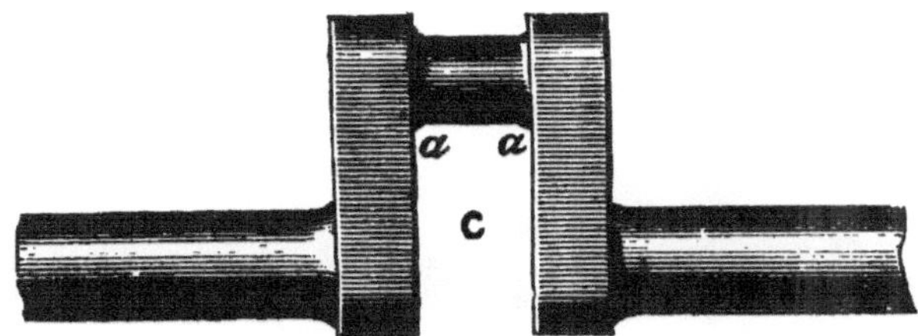

Fig. 98.—Slotted Crank.

The action of the fuller is typical forging, for it reduces the surface of the work without leaving angular marks upon its surface. It does not cut at all but leaves a wavy surface, with fibre perfectly continuous. When making a set off in a bar, whether with the object of reducing its dimensions or of bending it, the round-faced fuller is the tool that is used—never the keen chisel. The edge of the set hammer is also usually a little rounding, and does not form a sharp angle. The same applies also to most of the swages and other tools employed in working out forged forms.

The following figures illustrate in detail these remarks. The crank, Fig. 98, is forged as a solid block and slotted out at c, whilst the one shown in Fig. 99 is bent round or dipped. When the crank (Fig. 98) is slotted out, the crank webs, *a*, *a*, are weak, because the grain

or fibre runs in the direction of the engraved lines, and
the condition is quite analogous to the short grain in
wood. In Fig. 99 the fibre follows the contour of the dip

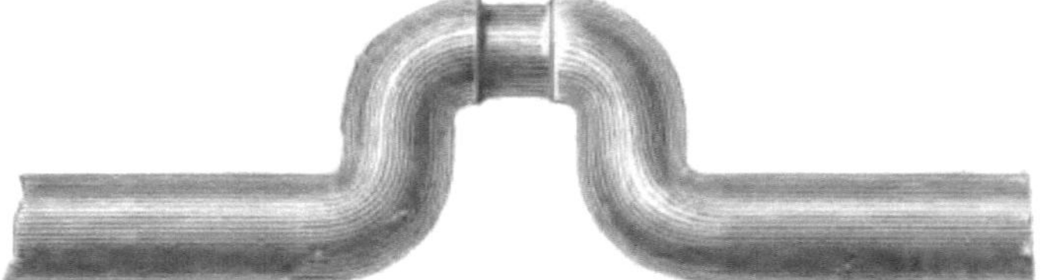

Fig. 99.—Bent Crank.

of the crank, and therefore the crank is of equal sectional
strength throughout. The weakness of the form, Fig.
98, is shown very forcibly in locomotive practice. The

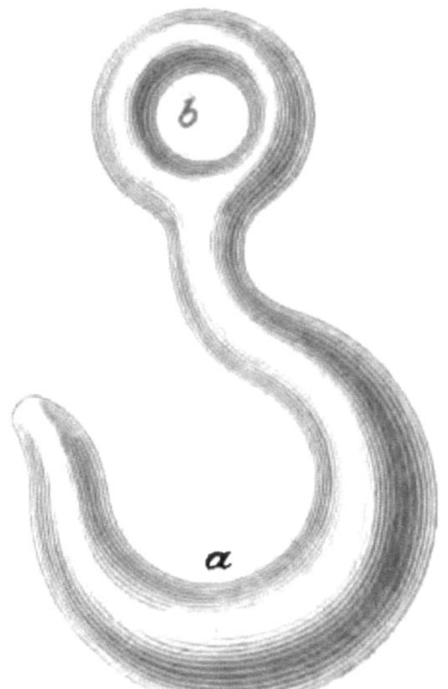

Fig. 100. Crane Lifting-hook.

cranks of inside cylinder engines are made in this
manner, and unavoidably so, because there is not room
enough to use a bent crank like Fig. 99; these cranks
invariably fracture at one of the webs (*a*) when
the engine has had a total run of about 200,000

miles. Frequently the webs break before that limit is reached, and for this reason the practice of bonding is now often resorted to. The crane lifting-hook, Fig. 100, is invariably bent round like the dip crank, and its sectional strength is preserved. If it were slotted the hook would break with much less strain.

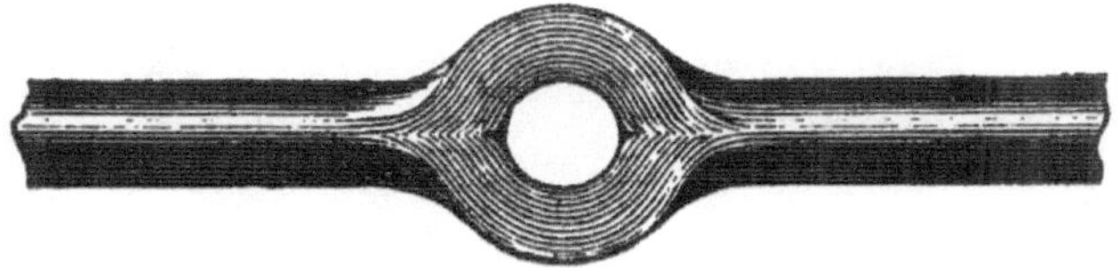

Fig. 101.—Punched Tie Rod.

Instead of drilling a hole for the eye *b* of this crane hook, it should be bent round and welded, or else punched. In drilling, the metal is severed; in punching, it is thrust aside and not divided. The punching preserves the continuity of the fibres, and, by bulging out the metal upon each side, preserves an equal section, and little or no jumping up is required. The punched rod (Fig. 101) is an illustration of the same

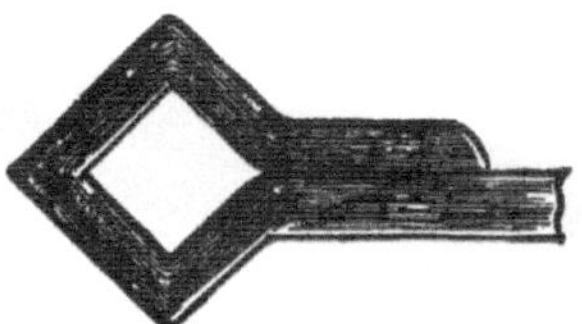

Fig. 102.—Welded Eye.

kind occurring in the middle of a bar, and is common in roof trusses.

The eyes of hammers, and the cottar ways in bolts and rods, should always be punched. There is then no separation, but only a parting or spreading of the fibres.

In forging the eye of a winch handle (Fig. 102), instead of making a solid end and drilling and filing a square hole, the bar is bent round a mandrel, and then welded.

Figs. 103, 104, and 105 show how the continuity of fibre is preserved in large forked ends. Small ends are usually shaped out of the solid but broad ends, like that illustrated, and also those of moderate width, are formed by dividing the bar and then opening it out. Fig. 103 shows the bar from which the forked end has to be made. A

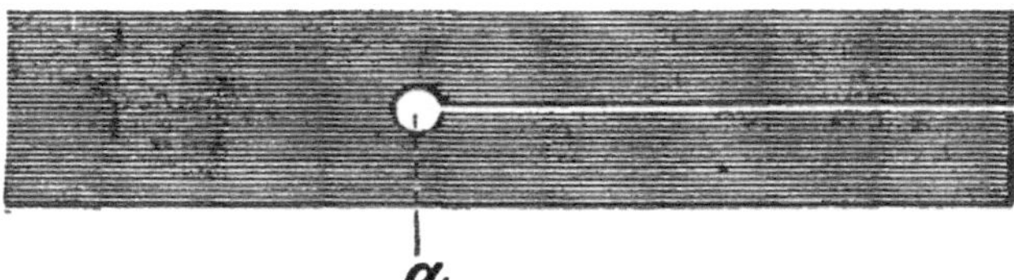

Fig. 103.—Bar divided with Hot Set.

hole is punched through at a ; this does not sever the fibre, but merely thrusts it sideways. Then the bar is divided with a hot set from the hole a outward to the end. The set is driven first from one face half-way through the bar, and then from the other face to meet in the middle. The punched hole prevents all risk of the

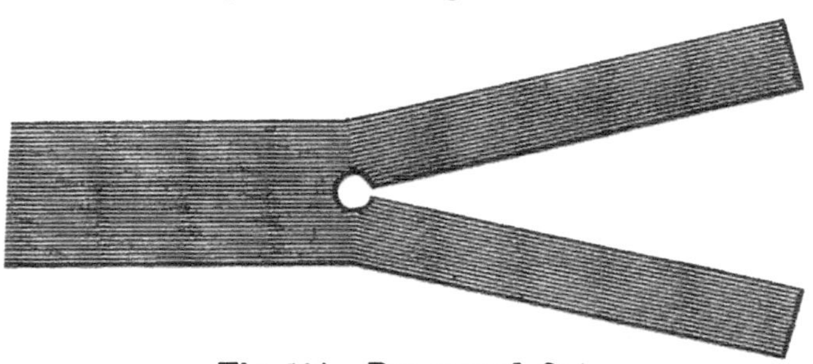

Fig. 104.—Bar opened Out.

set splitting the fibres inwards beyond the hole. Then the bar is opened out, first with a wedge, afterwards with the hammer, as in Fig. 104, and finally finished as at Fig. 105. If the fork were cut from the solid, the fibre would be short ; but being opened out and bent round, it runs continuously.

The direction in which the layers of iron occur has

frequently to be considered when making forgings. In a cottar key, for example, the layers of iron should

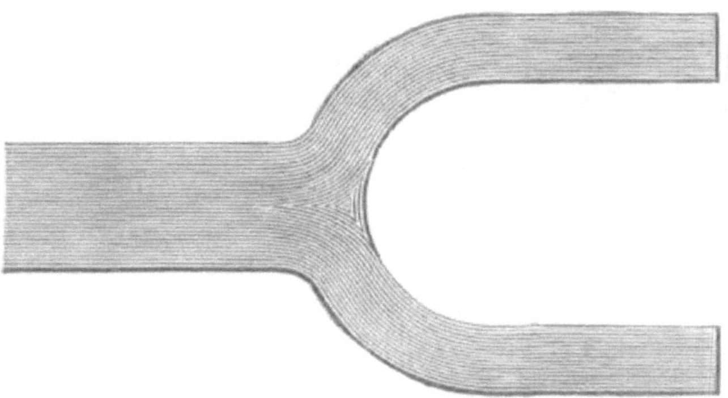

Fig. 105.—Finished Fork End.

be arranged, not in the direction of rotation of the shaft as in Fig. 106, as the pressure would tend to shear the key off in the plane of the layers, but at right angles, as

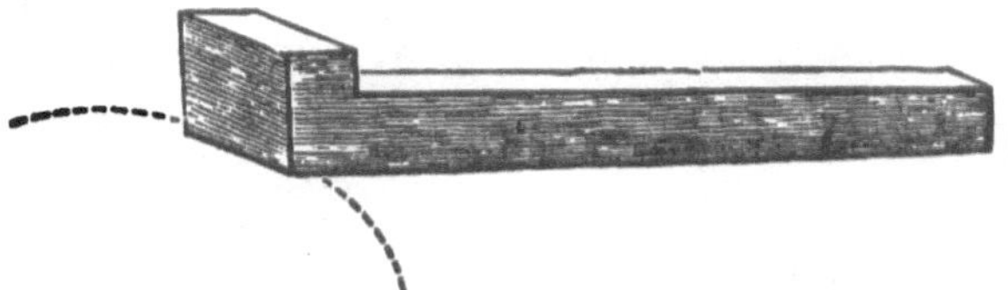

Fig. 106.—Key with Fibre Incorrect.

in Fig. 107, that is, the layers should radiate the centre of the shaft, so that the pressure will tend to close them. Nuts should be punched at right angles to the direction

Fig. 107.—Key with Fibre Correct.

of the fibre, otherwise the layers of iron are liable to become separated. The forked eccentric rod end (Fig. 108), forged solid and slotted out, should have the layers run not as engraved, but in the plane of the paper instead, otherwise the fibre is apt to open at *b*, and the forked end may fracture along *a, b*.

Liability to crack is much greater in inferior iron than in that of first-class quality. Lowmoor iron and the treble-best qualities of Staffordshire iron are comparatively close-grained and tough, but it is not

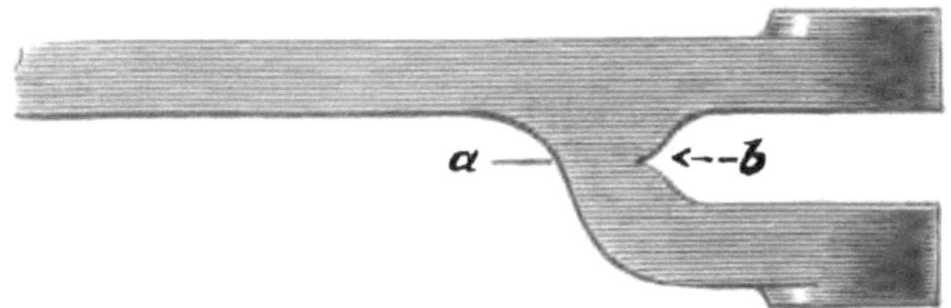

Fig. 108.—Forked End with Fibre Incorrect.

unusual when cut off with the hot set to find the bad qualities of iron showing cracks at the end (Fig. 109). These cracks are due to imperfect union, and to the presence of cinder, which has become intermixed with the iron and not expelled during the process of shingling. Sometimes hammering at a welding heat will

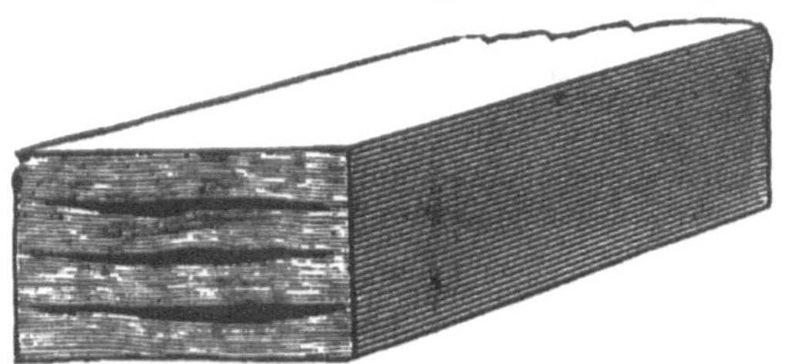

Fig. 109.—Cracks in Bad Iron.

improve such iron, but if the composition of the iron is bad, there is little advantage to be gained by this.

Anything that has to be screwed or subjected to great stress or wear, should be forged as sound and close-grained as possible by consolidation under the hammer, or between top and bottom tools at a welding heat. Otherwise the fibres may become partly separated and the metal frayed, so that the open texture of the iron will collect grit and wear rapidly.

CHAPTER VI.

BENDING AND RING MAKING.

THIS chapter will deal with some of the various methods employed in bending iron and in forming rings in that metal. Curves and rings of light section are easily bent over the beak of the anvil, or around a mandrel of suitable diameter. When the sections are heavy, bending blocks are necessary. It is easier to bend bar-iron flatwise than edgewise ; the reason is apparent if it is remembered that when a wide bar is bent two things happen. Along the centre of the bar (A, A, Fig. 110) there will be a neutral axis of metal that bends without

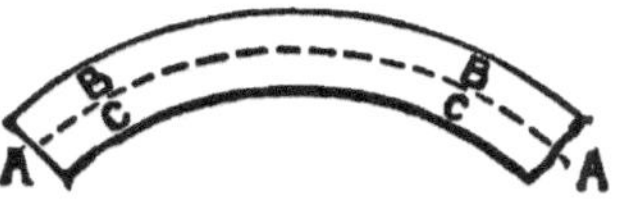

Fig. 110.—Diagram to Illustrate Tension and Compression.

compression or extension of fibre. But outside this neutral axis, the metal, B, B, is extended, and inside of this axis the metal, C, C, is compressed. The metal in tension and the metal in compression will seek relief from the intense stresses to which it is subjected. It will become wrinkled and puckered upwards and downwards. This tendency has to be corrected by hammering, or by the use of mechanical devices.

Many devices are resorted to in bending work of various sections and outlines. The making of a special cast iron templet, or bending block, is a question of relative cost. Where only a few plain pieces have to be bent, it will not pay to make the simplest block. Where there are many pieces, all alike, it pays to cast most elaborate blocks, and to fit them up with clips and cottars, or whatever may be necessary besides. It is usually easy for the smith to design blocks for forgings which he may require.

Fig. 111 shows a common type of block used for bending flat bars. Made in suitable sections, it is also often employed for bending T-iron. As shown, the working edge, A, is a circular arc; but it could be shaped to other curves equally well. The block has cast in it a stout cottared pin, projecting from its bottom face. This pin passes through a suitable hole in the levelling block, c, and is cottared beneath. For holding down cast-iron templet blocks, this is the most conve-

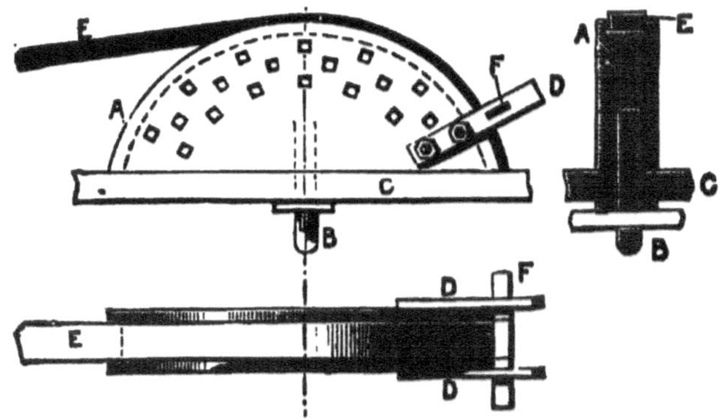

Fig. 111.—Bending Block.

nient method—better than having movable clips. One end, E, of the bar to be bent, is confined in its groove by clips, D, D. They are fastened with bolts through some of the holes, many of which are usually cast in all bending blocks, the cottar, F, passing through slot holes in D, D, holds the bar, E, down in its groove. As the free end of the bar, E, is bent farther round, more clips are brought to bear upon it, otherwise the bar could rise up from its seating.

Fig. 112 shows a common levelling and bending block fitted with a screw for general work. Upon it bars and plates of metal can be straightened and levelled by hammering. Forgings in process of formation can be tested from its face by the try-square, the back of it being laid upon the block and the blade against the vertical face of the work to be squared. The bevel gauge can be similarly used. Work can also be taken out of winding upon its surface; and it is used largely for bending iron bars to various curves. The block, A, is

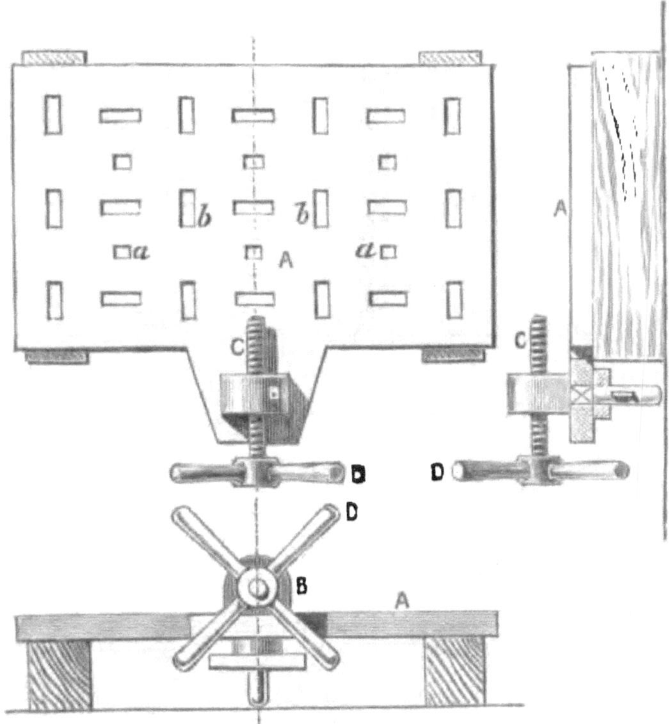

Fig. 112.—Levelling Block with Screw.

pierced with numerous circular and slotted holes, which receive pins forming the necessary supports for leverage when bending. There should be plenty of holes, but the plate should not be unduly weakened. At B there is a screwed block, secured to the plate with a shank or pin through which a cottar way passes. Driving in the cottar underneath secures this block in position, and by

F

the interposition or removal of a ring the height of the block can be varied. Through the block passes the powerful square-threaded screw, C, which is operated by the heavy cross handle, D. It is evident that if pins be

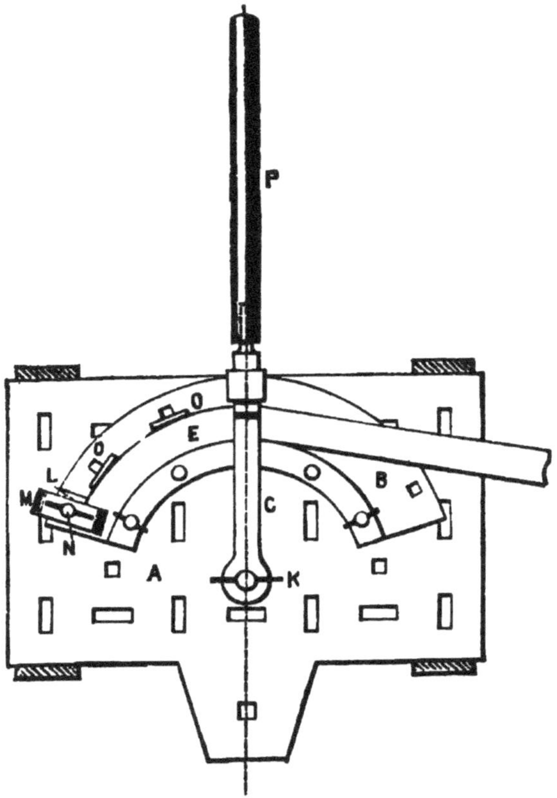

Fig. 113.—Front View of Levelling Block with Bending Templet.

inserted in holes, say at *a, a,* or at *b, b,* they will afford points of resistance to a bar that is laid against them when pressure is brought to bear about its central portions by the screw, C. As the ends of the bar cannot yield, it will be bent. By shifting the pins into other holes, the curvature of the bar can be varied.

Figs. 113 and 114 illustrate another method of making a ring upon the bending block, shown in Fig. 112. A is the block ; B is a templet casting, cottared down to the levelling block through the rough holes cast in the templet, the pins passing through any of the holes cast in the bending block that happen to be conveniently situated. The block is set so that its curvature follows round some particular hole in the bending block, in order that the radius bar or lever C, with its roller, D, may operate with equal pressure upon the ring, E, in every position. The lever moves upon a substantial pivot, F, whose shank or pin passes through the plate, and is cottared below. The detail of this fitting is shown in Fig. 115, where F is the solid body of the shank, whose pin, G, passes through the bending block, A. H is the pin upon which the bar, C, pivots, and J is a collar, of which one or more may be used for adjusting the height. K, K are top and bottom cottars.

One end of the bar, E (Figs. 113 and 114), to be bent is heated, and then secured at one end of the curved templet. As these templets are made

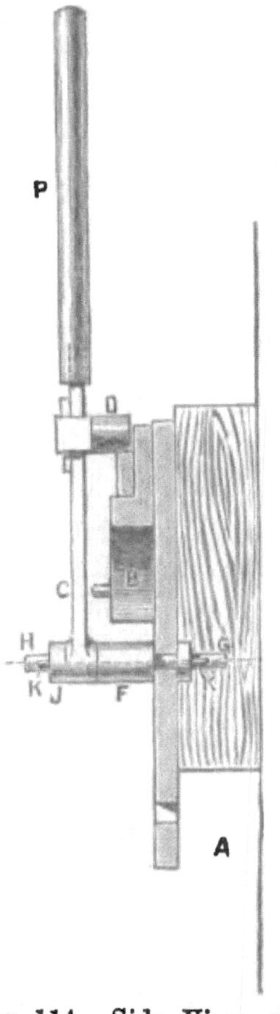

Fig. 114.—Side View of Levelling Block with Bending Templet.

specially to suit each job, and not for general work, it is usually practicable to cast a stop at the end where the bar is first secured. Such a stop is shown at L, Figs. 113 and 114, and in detail at Fig. 116.

This particular templet represents one used for making rings from which to cut the reversing links, of the type shown in Fig. 117, of the motion work of engines. Where such links are made in quantities, this is a cheaper method than forging and filing or machin-

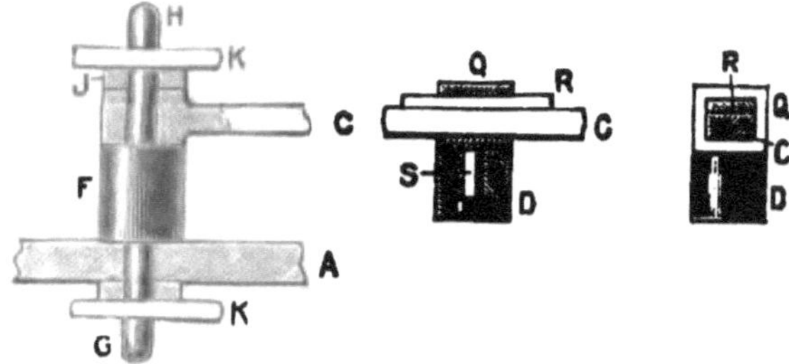

Fig. 115.—Details of Lever.

ing each link separately. Making a ring with radius equal to the curvature of the link, it is turned all over in the lathe, and then the separate links are slotted out of this ring, all being exactly alike.

In such a case as this, a flat oblong stop, L, Figs. 113 and 114, cast on one end of the templet block, is suitable.

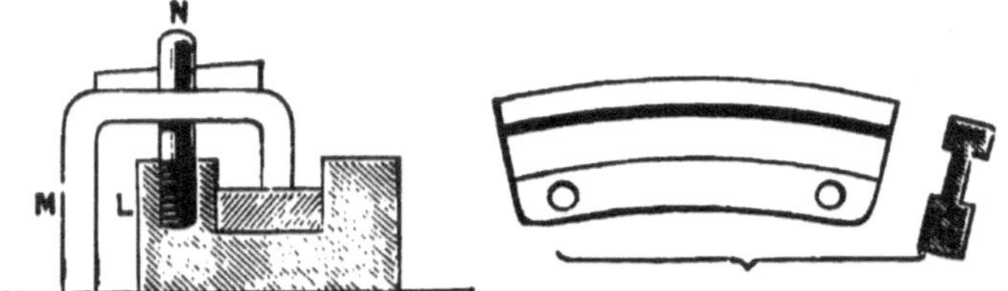

Fig. 116.—Details of Clip.   Fig. 117.—Reversing-link.

When bending a rigid bar, it is very difficult to get the extreme ends sufficiently curved. In this case the stop holds the end perfectly fast, and the curvature can be commenced from the very end. To prevent that end from rising during the process of bending, the clip, M (shown in detail at Fig. 116), is made to bear upon it. This is a piece of stout wrought iron pierced with a hole for the cottared pin, N, screwed into the bending templet. The long leg of the clip rests upon the face of the bending block ; the short leg is pressed upon the bar to be bent by the cottar ; the bar is thus pinched at one end.

The opposite end, if heavy, is supported by one of those appliances illustrated and described in Chapter I. A man, or two or three men if need be, stands at that end, and by main force pulls the bar round the curved templet, the supporting rest being moved along with the bar. The tendency of the bar to crumple up when the bending is taking place, is corrected by sledge hammer blows. Also to prevent the bar from becoming

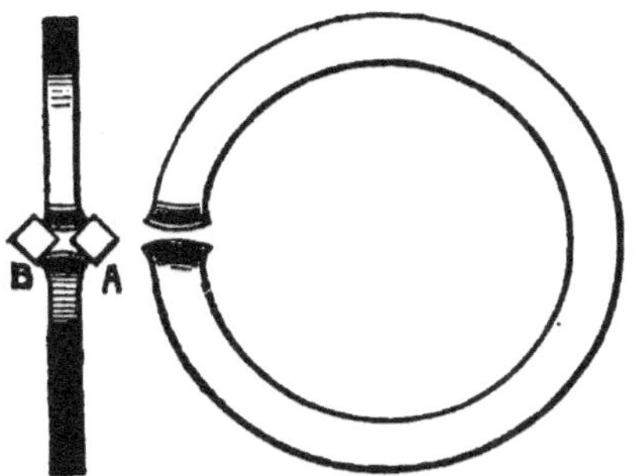

Fig. 118.—Method of Welding Ring.

unequally curved, pins are inserted at intervals in holes cast in the plate, and iron wedges, o (Figs. 113 and 114), are driven between these pins and the bar.

Much force is required to pull round the roller, D, against the edge of the iron. To avoid having a long lever which might be in the way, a bar, P, is often slipped over the end of the radius bar, C, and removed when not in actual use. The mechanism of the roller, D, is shown in detail in Fig. 115. Along the bar slides a block, Q, which may be fixed at any radius with the wedge, R. A stout bolt, S, is screwed into or forged on this block, and the roller, D, slips over it, and is held up by the nut underneath.

A heat cannot be taken over a great length in an ordinary forge fire. Therefore, after a short length, say from twelve to fifteen inches, of a bar is bent, it has to be released from the templet and put back into the fire to get the next section hot; and so on, until the entire ring is complete. Each time it is put back on the block, the portion already curved is secured with wedges. Sometimes also clips like M (Fig. 116) are cottared down over the bar to prevent it from rising.

When the circle is completed the ends have to be welded. The ends of the ring are upset before being brought together, and are spread in all directions. These upset edges are not welded together, but are united by "stick in" pieces. Into the V-like space formed on one side by the abutting ends, a square bar of iron, A (Fig. 118), is laid, and all being brought to the welding heat, a few blows of the hammer serve to unite

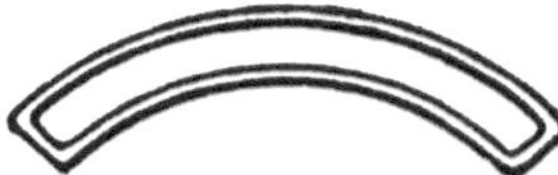

Fig. 119.—Iron Segment for Increasing Radial Capacity of Templet.

the bar and the ends of the ring. Any length of bar that happens to be handy is taken, and it is not at first cut off to the length required. One end only is brought to a welding heat, the opposite cold end serving as a porter. After the welding is completed, the end is cut off with the hot set. The ring is then turned over, and a similar "stick in" piece, B, is welded into the opposite V, precisely in the same fashion. The surfaces and edges are very rough and uneven; but the essential work is accomplished, and the rest is merely a matter of battering the faces with the flatter, and trimming the edges with the hot set and flatter. A heavy ring such as this cannot be manipulated easily until the smith's hands are relieved of its dead weight, so one of the appliances illustrated and described in Chapter L is used.

If a ring, or segment of a ring, is wanted only a few inches larger than the ring, B (Figs. 113 and 114), for which the templet was made, the smith, to save the expense of a new block, will make a filling-up piece (Fig. 119) of square bar.

Fig. 120 shows a block of a type useful when a large number of complete rings of the same size are required. The principle of its construction is very similar to that

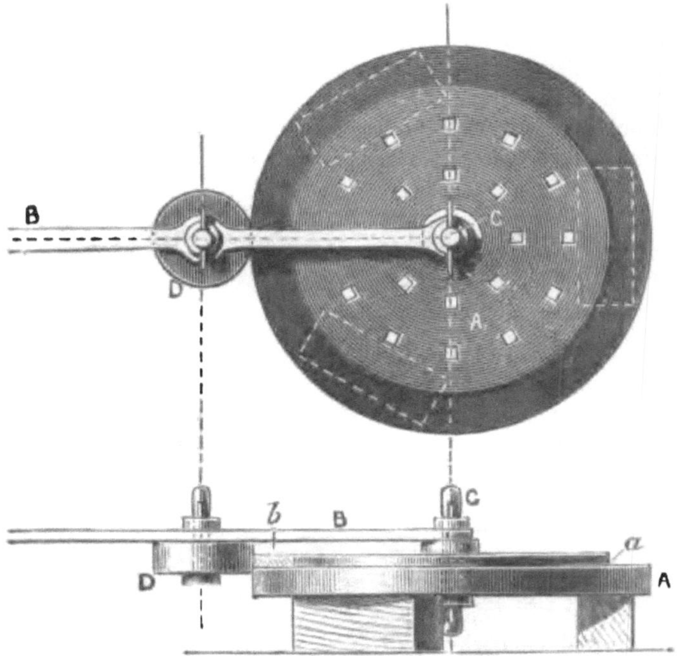

Fig. 120.—Circular Bending Block.

rigged up on the levelling block (Figs. 113 and 114); but in this case a complete circular disc, A, instead of a segment, is used. A lever, B, is pivoted in the centre of this disc by means of a cottar and pin, C, or a bolt. A roller, D, is pivoted on this lever. The ring is bent round the annular rebate, *a*, in the disc, and the roller, being pulled round with the lever, is pressed against the edge of the ring, which, confined between the roller, D, and the edge of a rebate on the disc, as shown by shading at *b*, cannot fail to become circular. The ring will have to be held down with clips, as in the previous example, for which purpose the holes cast in the central part of the disc are utilised in the way already described.

A templet like this can also be used for rings slightly larger in diameter and of different widths, by placing rings around the central portion, *a*, of the rebate, and by altering the diameter of the roller, D. It is, of course, not necessary that the periphery of the roller should coincide with that of the disc. If the ring to be formed is larger than the outside of the disc, then the

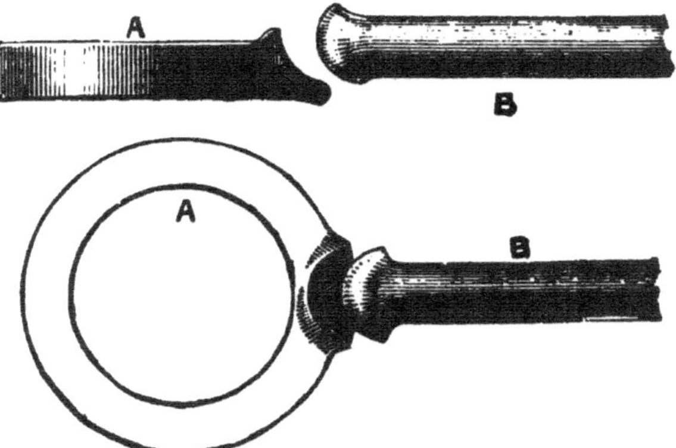

Fig. 121.—Welding Bridle to Spindle.

roller will be correspondingly smaller. If the ring is smaller than the disc, then the bottom of the roller will touch on the bottom of the rebated portion.

Slide-valve spindles of the bridle form are made in two or three ways. The bridle is sometimes circular, sometimes rectangular in shape, but the principle of its formation is the same. In the circular form the eye may be bent round and welded as a distinct ring, and the stem then welded to the eye ; by another method a portion only of the eye may be formed, and welded to another portion already made in one with a portion

of the stem ; by a third method the eye may be turned
round and welded from the bar which forms the stem.

Fig. 121 illustrates the first method. Here A is the
ring which has been upset, and scarfed, bent round on
the anvil beak, welded and fullered to receive the upset

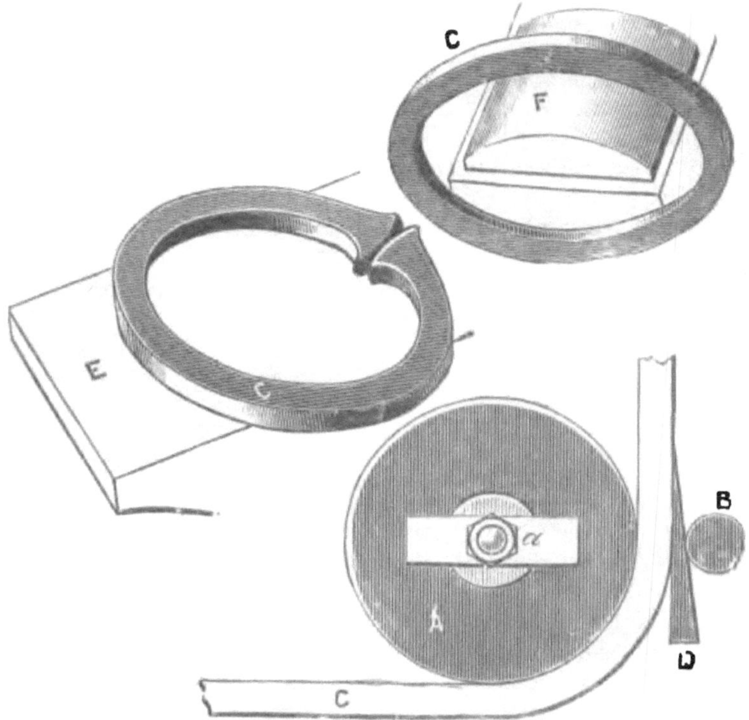

Fig. 122.—Method of Making Rings.

and fullered stem B, placed in position for welding.
The bar-iron from which the bridle, A, is made, is somewhat larger than the finished section—say $\frac{1}{8}$ in. each
way—and the ring is first bent round to a diameter
smaller than that of the finished ring. This allows
some finishing work to be done upon the bridle with
fullers and flatter, which will have the effect of reducing

the area and increasing the diameter. In this way the diameter of the ring may be increased to any reasonable extent, but it could not be reduced.

The ring is slipped over the anvil beak and its truth corrected with the hammer, or over a sugar-loaf-shaped casting (Fig. 20), flatters, fullers, and swages being employed for finally finishing the various flat and curved surfaces.

The bending of large bridles is best done in the manner shown in Fig. 122, and the same method is applicable to bending large rings in general. A cast-iron disc, A, of suitable size, and having a central hole, is bolted down on the face of a swage-block, the bolt *a* passing through one of the holes in the block. At a

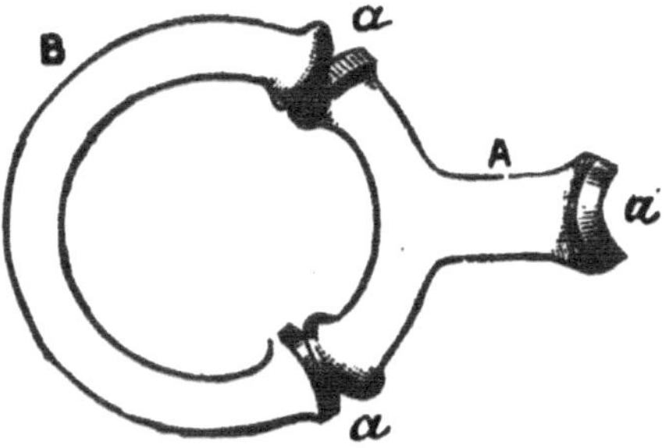

Fig. 123.—Method of Forming Bridle.

suitable distance a stop or pin, B, is inserted in another of the holes. The bar, C, to be bent is heated and placed between the disc A and the stop B, and is held securely with an iron wedge, D ; the free end is pulled round by hand if of sufficient length, or with tongs if short, and struck with the hammer the while to cause close bedding of the iron to the disc. When the ends of the intended ring overlap by an inch or two, it is removed, and the ends are scarfed and upset with the hammer or fullering tool, then welded upon the flat face of the anvil, E (Fig. 122), and finished upon a curved bolster, F, laid upon the anvil face, or provided with a shank to fit into the square hole in the anvil.

An alternative method (Fig. 123) of making the valve rod bridle is to take a rod of larger section than the valve rod, and fork one end by punching a hole and then driving in the hot set, first from one face,

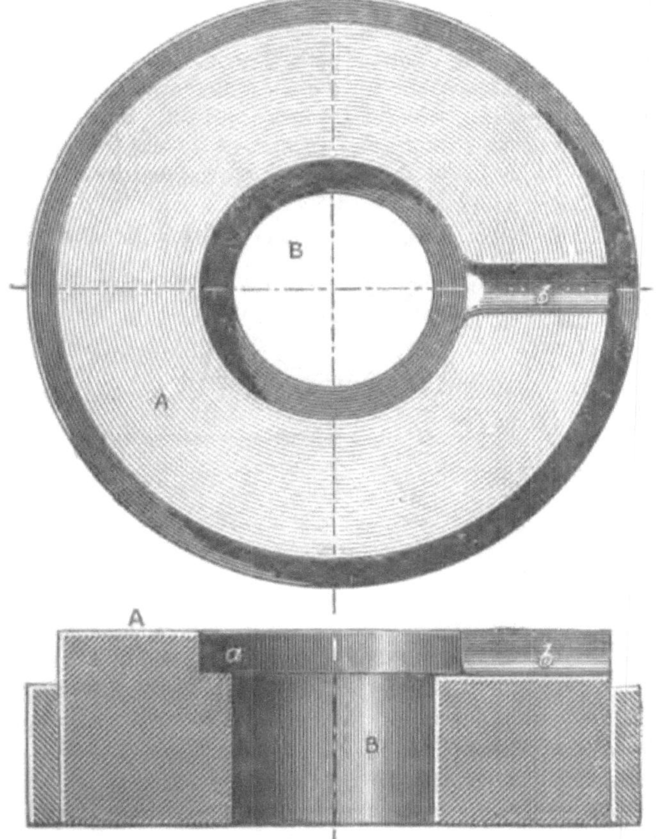

Fig. 124.—Die Block.

then from the opposite face, until the nicks meet in the centre of the bar. Open out the divided ends into a curved form, and reduce slightly, so as to approximate to the finished dimensions, leaving the

ends *a* (Fig. 123) of the original dimensions, and fullering them diagonally for scarfing (see A), which shows
the T-piece finished for welding). The iron, B, that is
to form the remainder of the ring, will be curved, and
fullered, and scarfed at the ends to match the T-
piece, A.

At this stage the ring will be less than the finished
diameter—say by about ¼ inch, dependent on the bulk
of the work—to allow for working and finishing subsequent to welding, which stretches the iron. The spindle
will be welded with a scarfed joint on to the free end *a*,
or if the spindle is short it may be drawn down from
the T-piece itself.

Where many bridles are made alike for standard

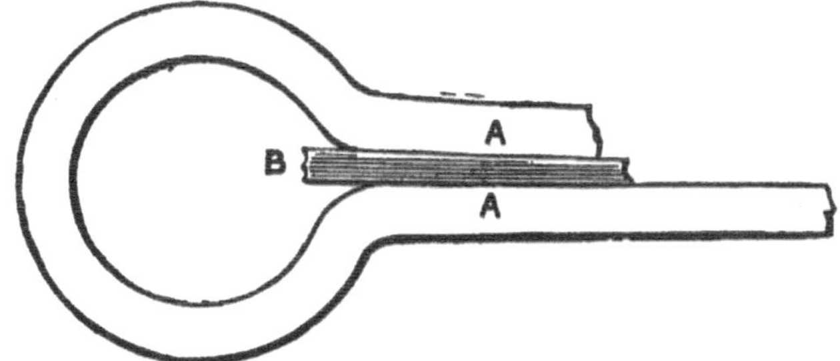

Fig. 123.—Method of Forming Bridle.

engines, a die block is employed for final finishing. Its
shape is shown at Fig. 124. A is of cast iron, cored or
bored out at *a* for the bridle, and cored out at *b* for the
stem to lie in ; B is a central steel plug or pin, the size of
the hole in the bridle. The bridle is hammered into
the die with a couple of blows of the steam hammer,
next the die is turned upside down on a suitable
bolster, and the pin B and the forging struck out at a
blow. Then the pin is released from the forging, and
the bridle is finished, except for cutting off with a set
the fins around the top edges.

Fig. 125 shows the third method, in which the bar
is bent round and welded at A. To preserve the
continuity of the circle, a glut or wedge-piece, B, is

inserted in the weld. Without this, by this method it would be difficult or impossible to form a perfect internal curve. The finishing of the bridle by means of tools and of dies, differs in no respect from that of the previous example.

The mode of making a rectangular bridle, unless of small dimensions, would be that shown in Fig. 126. Two T-pieces, A, A, are formed by division similarly to the T-piece A in Fig. 123, and the remainder of the

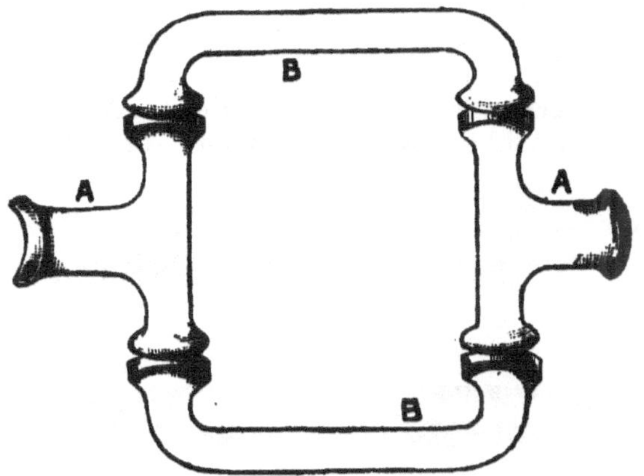

Fig. 126.—Method of Forming Rectangular Bridle.

rectangle is formed of the two pieces, B, B, bent round and scarfed to meet the scarfed ends of the T-pieces. The rods may be drawn down from the ends of A, A, or welded on.

When a smith wants bending blocks of the kind mentioned in this chapter, it is as well to know that complete wooden patterns are seldom made for them. A pattern segment of the block given to the iron-moulder, with a sketch or drawing of the complete block, with suitable instructions, is all that is required. The moulder will place any number of plain cores in the mould for the pin-holes.

CHAPTER VII.

MISCELLANEOUS EXAMPLES OF FORGED WORK.

THE subjects now to be treated will embrace some of the common types of forgings, such as rods, levers, and bolts, made and used in the construction of machinery. Rods and links with bosses, like Fig. 127, are used extensively in various forms and proportions. At first sight, upsetting would appear to be the most ready method of

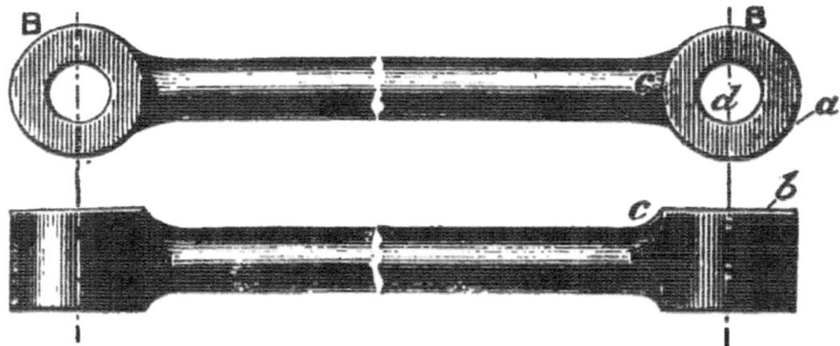

Fig. 127.—Rod or Link with Bosses.

making such rods. It seems simple to take a rod or bar, as the case may be, the size of the intermediate portion A and to dump up the ends to make the bosses B. But upsetting tends to open or spread the grain and to impair its continuity, and the operation would require several heats, and occupy much time, unless the bosses were very small.

There are three types at least :—(1) When the bosses are small relatively to their rods, and the rods are only a few inches long, as in some machinery links and levers, it is practicable, though not desirable, to form them wholly by upsetting. Properly, they should be made either by partial upsetting and partial drawing

down, or wholly by drawing down, according to the stock
that happens to be used. (2) When the bosses are
relatively large and the eyes relatively small (Fig. 128)
and the rods are several feet in length, as in the tie rods
of roofs, they may be forged from the solid, apart
from their rods, and welded on. (3) When the eyes are

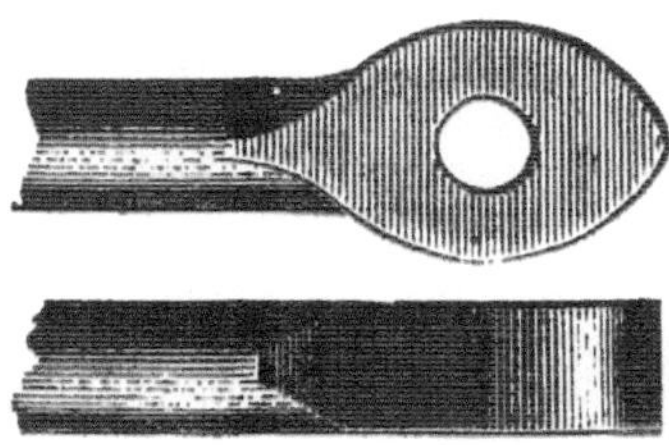

Fig. 128.—Small Tie Rod.

large (Fig. 129), as in the truss and tie rods of bridges,
jibs of travelling cranes, etc., they may be formed by
bending round and welding the iron, and usually also
by welding the eyes to their rods.

All these will be finished after rough hammering
by the aid of the hollow top and bottom tools or swages,
operating on the curved edges (*a*, Fig. 127); by the flatter

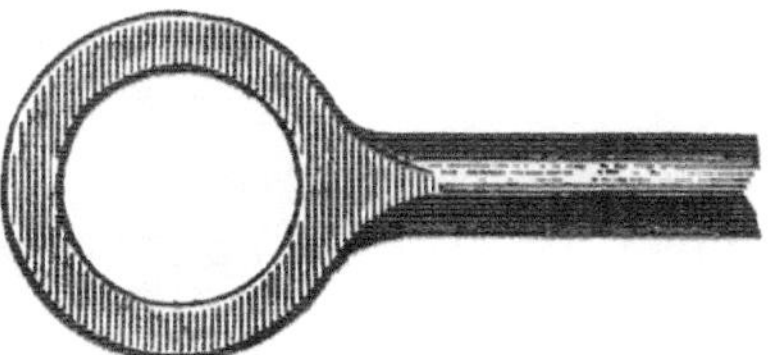

Fig. 129.—Large Tie Rod.

and sledge on the flat faces *b*, and by the fullering tool
around the neck *c*. In repetition work the eyes would
be finished in a pair of cast-iron dies, like Figs. 130 and
131 ; the former gives the finished curvature to the
edges *a* and the fullered neck *c*, whilst the latter
completes the flat faces *b* in succession. The eye *d* is
punched while the boss B lies in the die, the core falling
down into the hole A, a trifle larger than the punch.

The boss is beaten into the dies with the sledge, or preferably under the drop, or the steam hammer.

These blocks are made of square as well as of circular form, but the latter is to be preferred, because of the greater ease experienced in fitting and shrinking on the bond shown in Figs. 130 and 131, where B is a wrought-iron bond shrunk on to prevent the cast iron from bursting from the concussion to which it is subject.

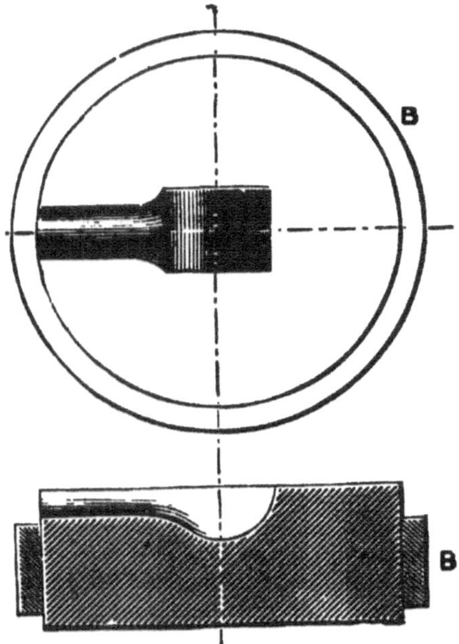

Fig. 130.—Die Block.

Dies like this are often made in pairs, top and bottom being coupled with pins for use under the steam hammer.

(2) The bosses are made from bar iron of their own dimensions, and a sufficient length is drawn down—say from three to six inches—to permit of making, with the long plain body of the rod, a scarfed welding joint (Fig. 132).

(3) The eye is bent round and welded, forming a short solid shank, which is then scarfed and fullered for

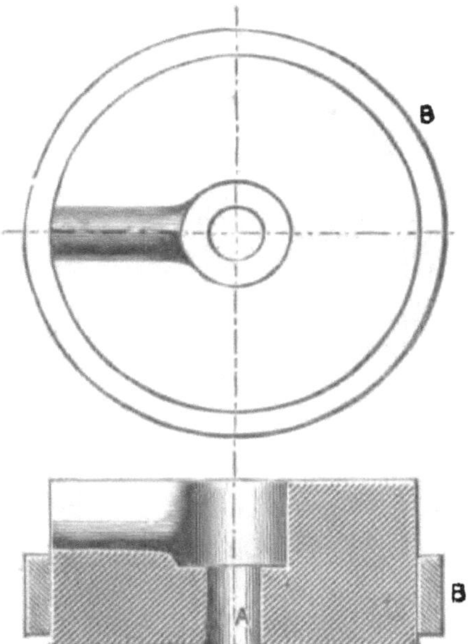

Fig. 131.—Die Block.

welding, like Fig. 133. Or it is bent round to form a tongued joint (Fig. 134), in which a wedge-like end is fitted into a corresponding cleft, and welded. This is

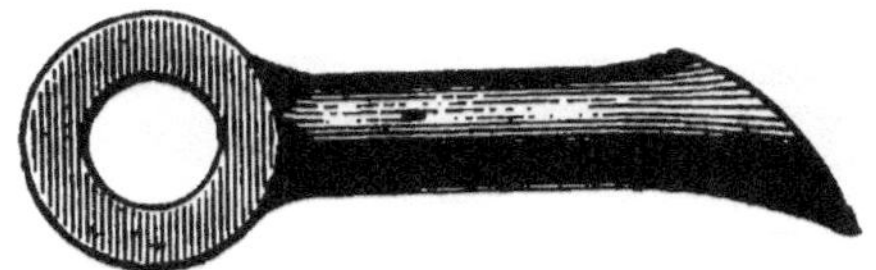

Fig. 132.—Boss End Scarfed for Welding.

supposed to be stronger than the plain scarf, and is often used for iron of heavy section.

Fig. 135 shows a tongue joint in solid bars. To make it, first upset both ends; then for the tongue A set in a fullering tool on opposite sides of the upset portion (Fig. 136, *a*). Then, by hammering, the end will be tapered down until it has the appearance of Fig. 135, A. For the recess B, nick the other upset end inwards with a chisel, and open out sufficiently with a wedge.

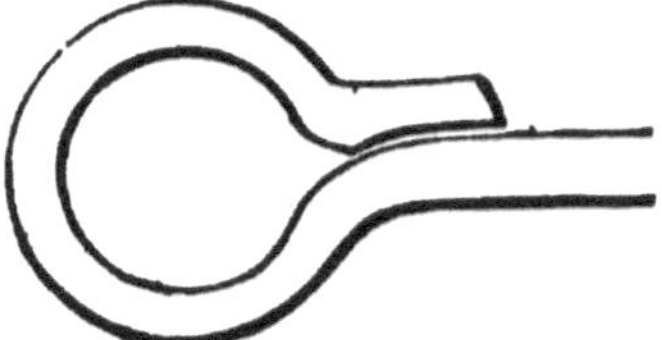

Fig. 133.—Eye bent for Welding.

This will spread the end more, as well as open it out ; and this spreading out is an advantage, because it gives plenty of metal for welding and swaging down to finished dimensions. The tongue joint is then made in

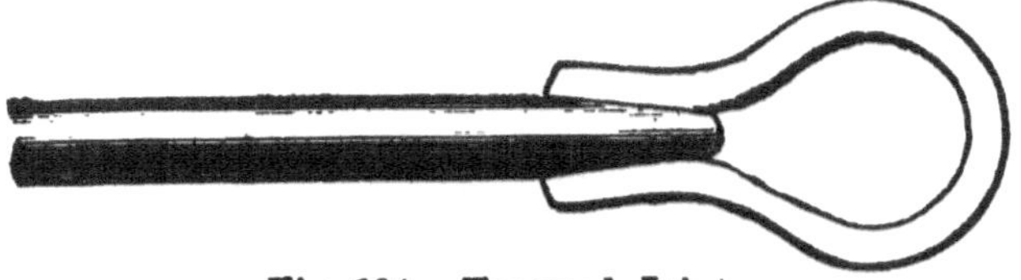

Fig. 134.—Tongued Joint.

the usual way by heating both ends to the welding heat, and when assured that the faces are free from dirt and scale, closing them together, first with the hammer, and finishing them with the top and bottom swages. To

Fig. 135.—Solid Tongued Joint.

ensure union at the termination of the tongue, the first blows should be given endwise. These may be given while the work is in the fire, provided the fire is clean, and the joint cleansed by throwing sand into the fire over the work. When the circumference of the joint is being hammered, the angular swages may be used to better advantage than by merely laying the work upon the anvil.

Levers of the general form shown in Fig. 137, but

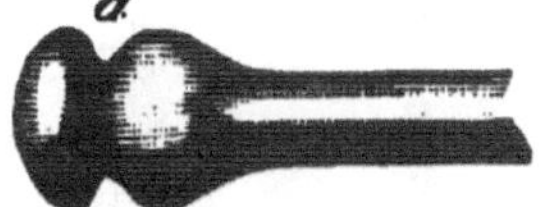

Fig. 136.—Fullered End.

variously proportioned, are very common. The methods of forging them will be modified by circumstances. They may be drawn wholly from the solid, or partly

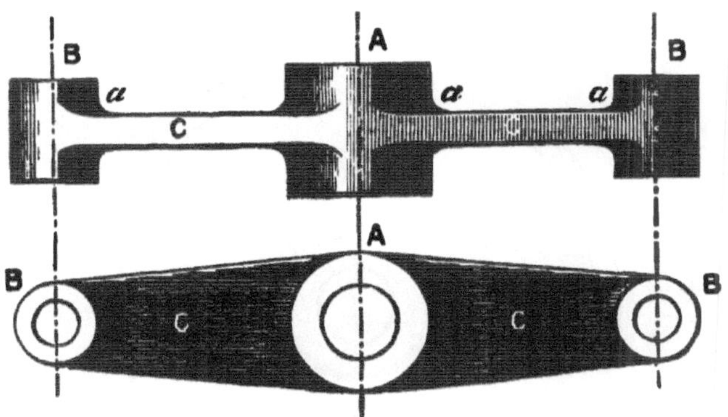

Fig. 137.—Double-ended Lever.

drawn and partly welded—seldom, however, being upset.

A lever of the proportions shown in Fig. 137 would, in

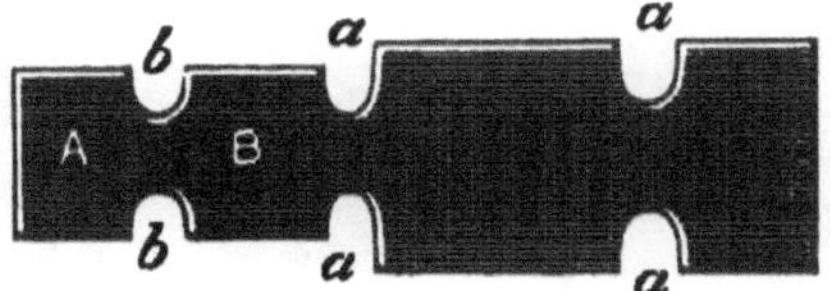

Fig. 138.—Fullered Lump.

general, be formed wholly by drawing down. A bar of iron, having a sectional area about equal to that of the central boss A, is selected. First, a fuller is

driven in on opposite sides, as at *a, a, a, a* (Fig. 138).
Then the bar is drawn down roughly from the fuller
nicks to the ends, until the ends are reduced to an area

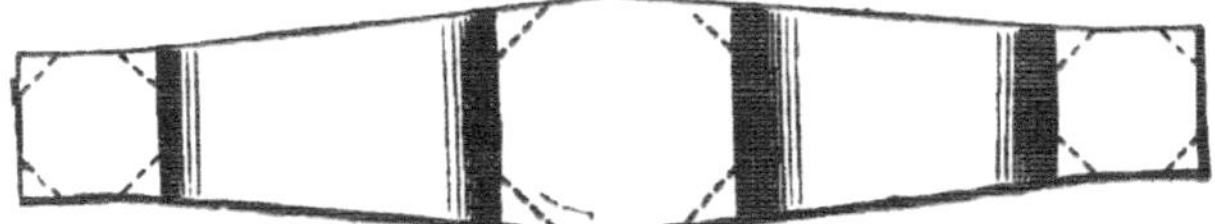

Fig. 139.—Lever Roughly Forged.

A (Fig. 138), suitable for the smaller end boss B (Fig. 137).
Again the fuller is driven in at *b, b* (Fig. 138), and then

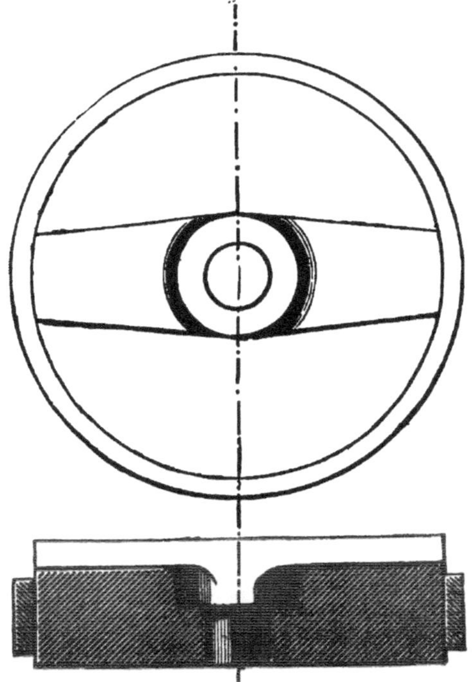

Fig. 140.—Die Block.

the intermediate portion B is reduced by fullering or by
hammering until the required thickness of the web
(c in Fig. 137) is nearly reached. The blows are delivered

on sides and faces alternately, drawing the sides to the tapered form seen in the plan view, as well as the webs to thickness.

There is no attempt at finish just yet, for the centres of the bosses are probably not the correct size, and it will

Fig. 141.—Fullered Lump.

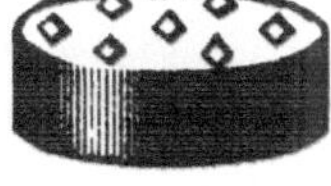

Fig. 143.—Boss Lump prepared for Dabbing On.

very likely happen that some further drawing down, or even some upsetting, will be required before the boss lumps will be sufficiently near to correct centres, to permit of their finishing to the required dimensions. Rough measurement will be taken from time to time with the rule, or with some form of gauge.

At this stage the lever will resemble Fig. 139,

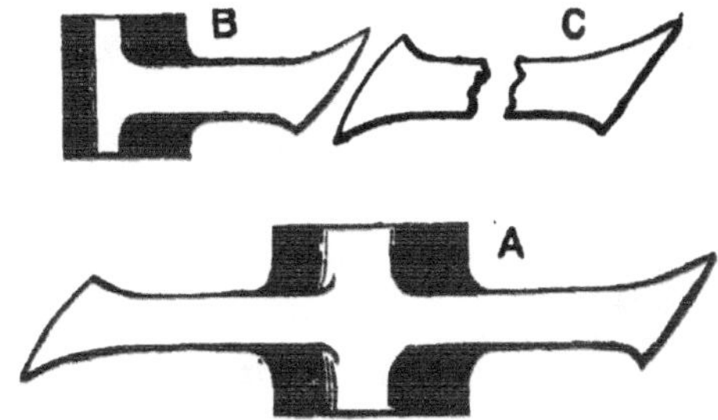

Fig. 142.—Bosses and Rod Scarfed for Welding.

with square lumps at centre and ends of the webbed portion. To hammer these bosses into a circular form would involve much labour and several heats, so the corners are cut off with a hot set, as shown by the dotted lines. When a boss is small, four corners only are cut off; when large, eight, or even more. The set is driven perpendicularly first, but not right down to the web, it stops at the radius or hollow—and then horizontal cuts are made to meet the perpendicular ones, and so the boss is rudely chiselled to a circular form. Then the hammer, and afterwards the hollow swage, are used to give a more circular form to the bosses ; and the hollows shown at *a*, *a*, in Fig. 137 are shaped with a hollow fuller. Thus bosses can be made fairly shaped, but not perfectly

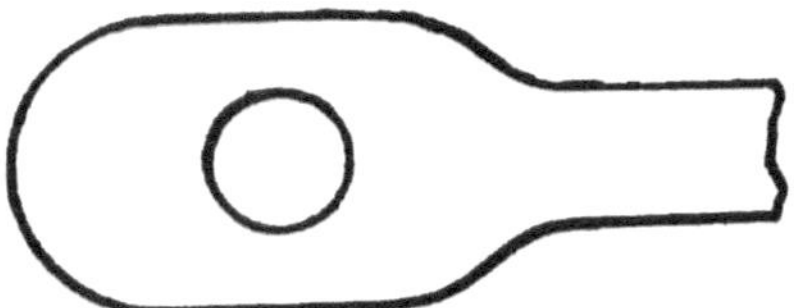

Fig. 144.—Tie Rod End.

true. In repetition work dies are used ; that for the end bosses would be like Fig. 131, and these (B in Fig. 137) would be hammered into a recess in the middle of the die, and the web would rest in a recess reaching from the centre to the outside. The die for the centre boss is shaped like Fig. 140. Bosses finished thus are so true that they can be eft without subsequent turning, brightening on the emery wheel giving sufficient finish.

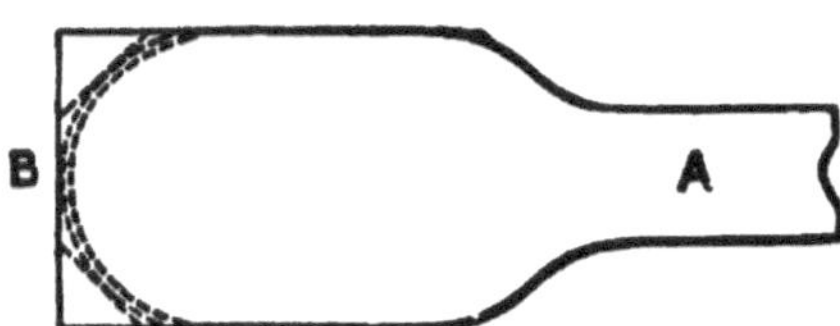

Fig. 145.—Rough Forging for Tie Rod End.

For a lever anything over a foot in length, it would be easier to take separate pieces of bar iron for the web, and separate pieces for the bosses, and weld them together. Thus a lump (Fig. 141) would be taken for the central boss, and set in with the fuller at *a*, *a*, and drawn down at each end, *b*, *b*, leaving the extreme ends rather thicker than the intermediate portion, A, Fig. 142, in order to form scarfed joints for welding. The end bosses, B, would be similarly prepared, and all welded to the webs, c, which is also upset and scarfed. The shaping and finishing of the bosses are most conveniently done before the welding up.

Another way is to weld or "dab" bosses on the web; these are cut off an iron rod of suitable diameter. The red-hot boss (Fig. 143) is roughed with a corner of the chisel, which is held diagonally and struck with a hammer. These roughings assist the union of the welded surfaces, which being then raised to a welding heat, the flat bars and the bosses are made to adhere by

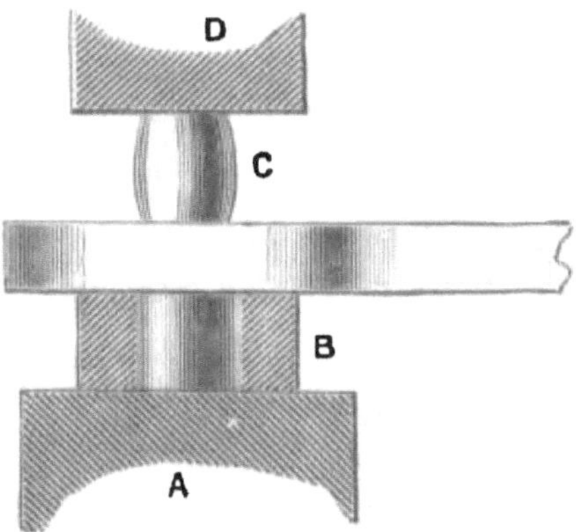

Fig. 146.—Punching Hole in Tie Rod End.

a few hammer blows. The thinner the web, the more intimate and secure the weld.

When forging articles in this way, it will be necessary to test the parallelism and the rectangular form, and the winding of the various parts. Forgings are apt to develop inaccuracy quickly while the metal is soft, so the smith employs the eye in these early stages of the work, and squares, and calipers, and straight-edges as it becomes cooler.

Large tie-rod ends (Fig. 144) are always welded to their rods. A rectangular lump is drawn down (Fig. 145) at the end A to a trifle larger than the rod, and scarfed for welding. The corners B are rounded by first cutting off the angles with the hot set, and then by rounding off with the chisel shown at Fig. 51. In these rods the eyes, being large, are usually punched first, and frequently they are reamered out afterwards. Such large holes are punched with difficulty under the sledge, but easily under the steam hammer. Fig. 146 shows the arrangement employed : A is the anvil of the steam hammer, and upon this rests the bolster, B, which must be sufficiently large to give proper bearing support to the eye, and its hole must be a trifle larger, but not much larger than that of the punch C. Two or three blows of the hammer or

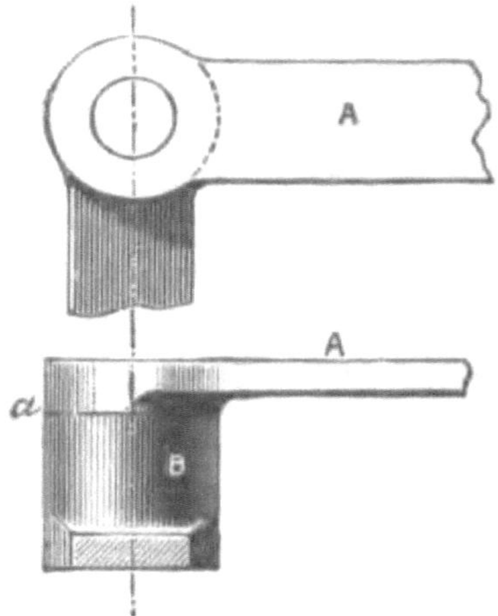

Fig. 147.—Lever Arms.

tup, D, will drive the punch through ; this is slightly bellied in order to squeeze the metal, and also to clear itself of the hole easily.

After rounding the edges and punching the hole, but before the bar is quite cool, the flatter will be used to smooth over the edges that have been slightly upset during these processes.

Often the arms of bossed levers stand at an angle with each other, and also are not in the same plane, and then the methods previously described are not applicable. Fig. 147 shows a portion of a lever, with arms placed on opposite sides of the boss at right angles to each other. There are two ways in which these levers may be attached to the boss. One by "dabbing on"— that is, the arm A, with a portion of the boss, is welded flat upon the main portion of the boss B, along the plane *a*, the surfaces being first hatched over with the corner of a set ; by the other way (Fig. 148), one side of the boss if fullered, as at A, with a round-faced fuller, the end of the lever arm B is upset, and the two welded together. This is a very common method of welding. The fuller not only indents the boss, but, by means of blows delivered diagonally, is made to throw up the metal all around in a ridge, thus giving some extra metal for

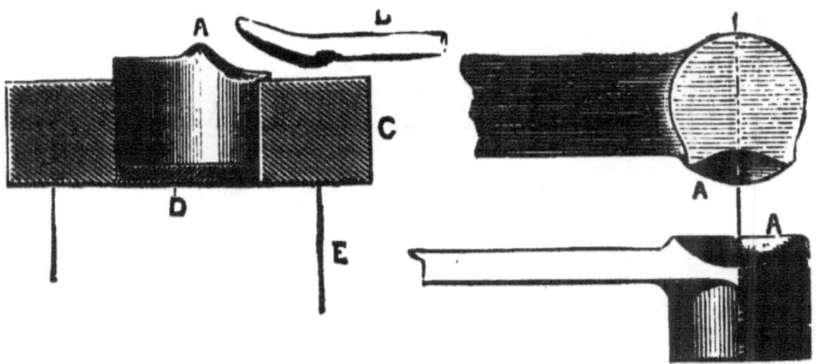

Fig. 148.—Welding on Arm.

finishing off. In Fig. 148, C is a die-block, in which the boss is held while the arm is being welded ; D is a thickness piece, or washer ; and E is the anvil. If no die-block is available, the boss will be held with open-mouthed tongs of globular form.

Eccentric and valve rods afford some typical examples of engine forgings. The eccentric rod (Fig. 149) is usually made in two pieces, and welded at about the centre ; or, if rather long, the ends are welded to a central plain bar.

The extreme dimensions of the end A represent roughly the original size of the bar, from which the shank B is drawn down. From that original bar there is swaged down a length sufficient for welding. The

large end is cut off to the precise length required with
the knife tool, or with the curved knife if the steam

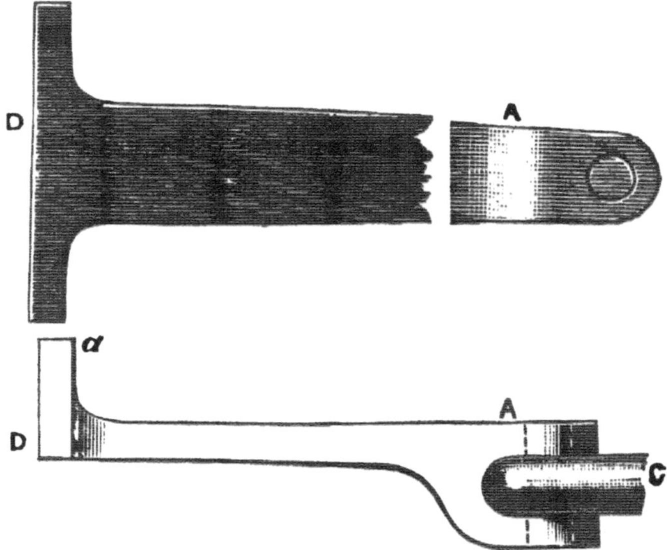

Fig. 149.—Eccentric Rod.

hammer is used, or with a hot set if power is not
available. Then it is necessary to cut off upon the
anvil any sharp corners with a cutting-off tool, giving

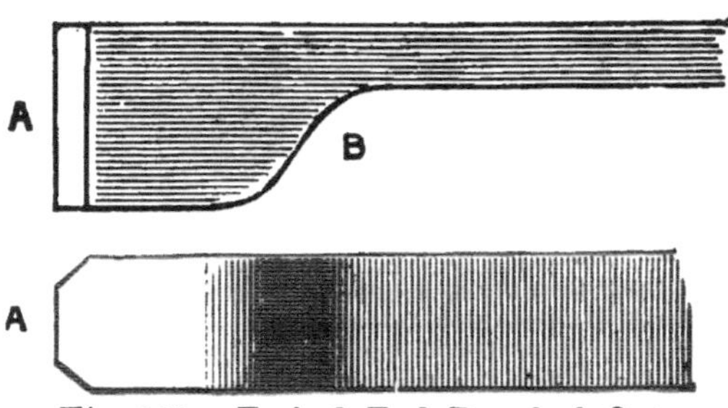

Fig. 150.—Forked End Roughed Out.

the appearance of Fig. 150, and swage the end A, rounding with a hollow swage, letting the shoulder B lay
against the beak of the anvil, and finally, to finish in a

die-block (Fig. 151). Of course, the die-block is used for finishing only when the quantity of forgings required is sufficient to pay for its cost.

The body A of the block is of cast iron, and a wrought iron ring B is shrunk on. The recess C, it will

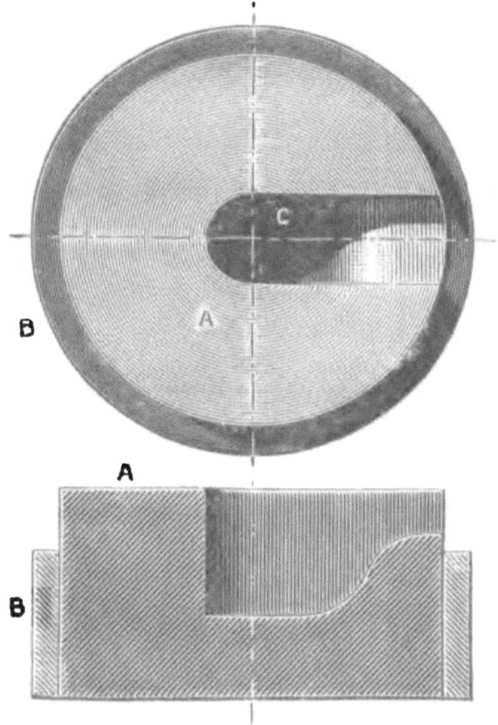

Fig. 151.—Die Block.

be seen, corresponds with the outline of the end A in Fig. 149.

Another way to forge the forked end is to take a bar about half the thickness of the forked end, and double the iron over, and weld a length that will extend rather farther than the termination of the radius.

In both of these methods the gap may be cut out roughly by the smith or left to be machined out. The general methods of forming forked ends have already been described, and now it is only necessary to show by a sketch how forked ends, whose gaps are formed by forging, and not by machinery, are shaped. After the metal has been cut out from the gap and roughly brought to form, a filler, shown shaded at c, Fig. 149, is inserted, and while this remains in, the outside of the

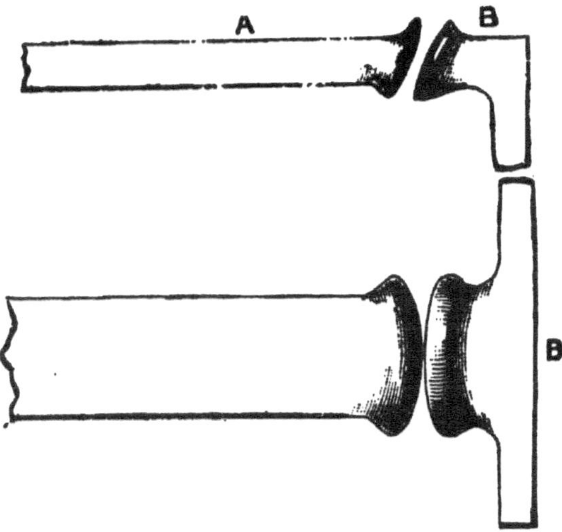

Fig. 152.—Welding Flat End of Eccentric Rod.

forked end is finished with flatter and hollow swage. The filler usually has a square shank to fit the square hole in the anvil.

The end D in Fig. 149 is made by one of three methods. Either the shank B is fullered down from a bar of the original section of the end D ; or the shank A (Fig. 152) is welded to a piece of flat bar B, of the dimensions of the end D in Fig. 149 ; or the end of a bar is divided and opened out. The first method is not correct because the iron fibres are short, but it is often adopted, as there is not very much stress on the flat end when bolted up to the eccentric straps, and the hammering it receives at the welding heat helps to consolidate the metal.

The second method has the advantage of preserving the best arrangement of the fibres. In it, the flat piece B (Fig. 152) is fullered and upset with a round-faced

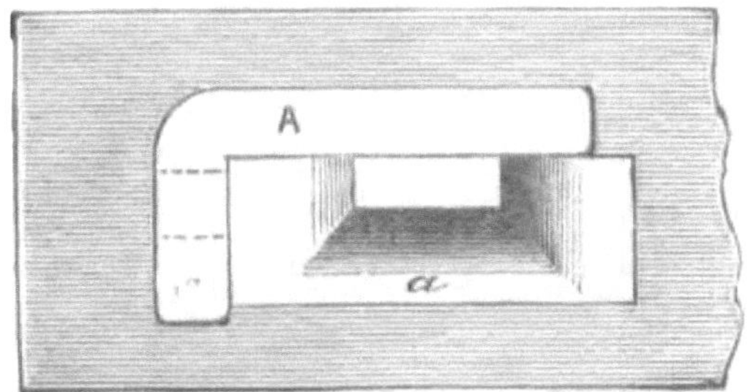

Fig. 153.– Anvil Stop.

fuller, and the end A, similarly fullered, is welded to it. In either case, to permit of finishing off, the iron selected is a trifle larger in section than the finished section. Where the shank is drawn down from the solid, a good deal of finish on face a (Fig. 149) has to

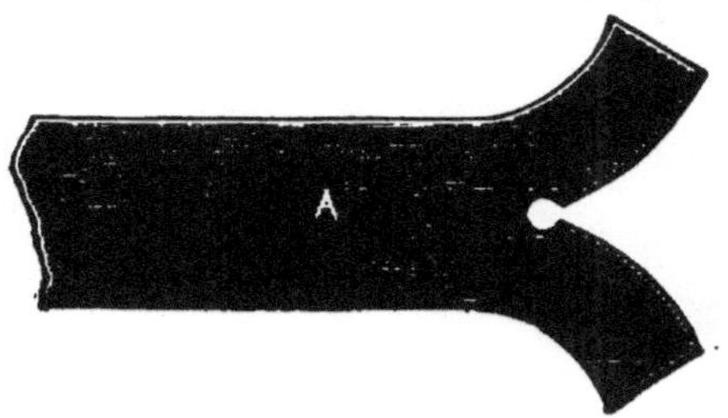

Fig. 154.—Opening Out End of Bar.

be done with the flatter, the rod being held vertically with the face D upon the anvil face. To prevent the rebounding backwards of the forging, in consequence of the edge of the flatter striking the shank, a bent bar of iron (Fig. 153, A) is fitted with a shank into the hole on the anvil face. The flatting of the inner face a of course has a tendency to spread the edges and bulge them in some places, and this is corrected with blows on those edges from the hammer and from the flatter.

The third method of forming the flat end is by forking the end of a stout bar in the fashion shown in

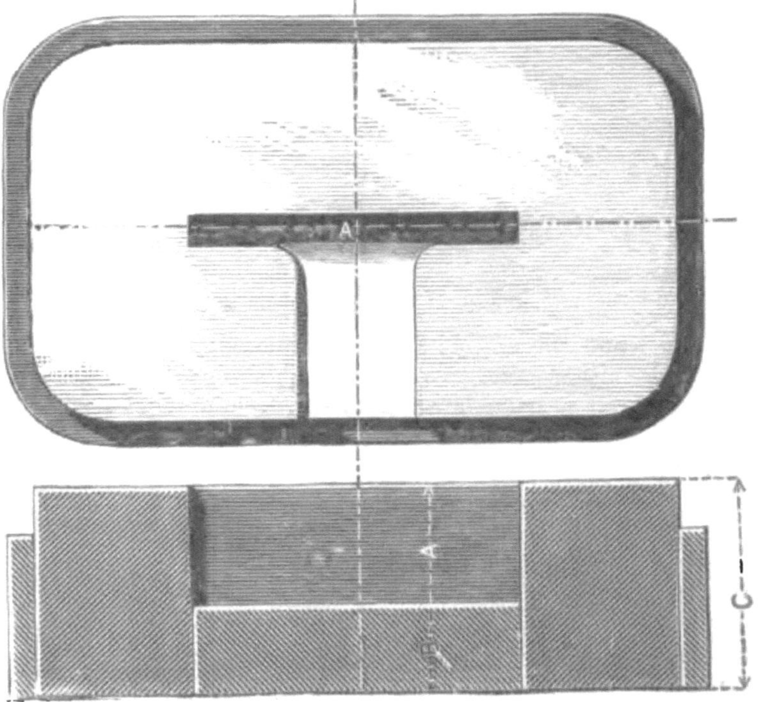

Fig. 155.—Die Block.

Fig. 154, and opening the ends outwards. Continuity of fibre is thus preserved. The end A is fullered down thinner, and drawn out, and then cut off the main bar, whose length may serve as a porter, and scarfed for welding to the stem.

When these rods are made in quantities, the final finish is imparted in a cast-iron die of the form shown in Fig. 155, in which A is the recess that gives the flat end its perfect finish, and B a flat piece of steel, whose depth makes up the precise difference between the depth c and of the flat end A, and by means of which the T-end is driven out of the die immediately after it is moved off the anvil block of the steam hammer. The block being turned upside down, a blow or two on the piece B drives the finished T-piece out from the die.

When the fins formed at the edges are being cut off with the set, the forging is placed upon a piece of sheet iron, bent over at the ends to clip the edges of the anvil. This sheet of iron prevents the cutting edges of the set from becoming dulled by contact with the hard steel face of the anvil.

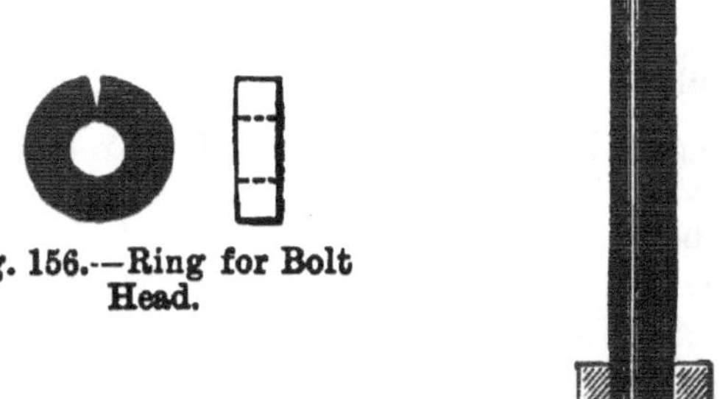

Fig. 156.—Ring for Bolt Head.

Fig. 157.—Rod driven into Ring.

Bolts and nuts are bought more cheaply than they can be forged in small quantities, and they are consequently seldom made in smiths' shops. But a description of their manufacture is not superfluous, because in it are illustrated several facts that find useful application in other classes of work.

In making bolts there is the choice of three methods. In one, a bar is selected of about the size of the bolt head across the angles, and the stem is drawn down, first roughly by the hammer, and then between swages.

Another method is to take a bar of the diameter of the bolt and upset a mass of metal to form the head. Neither of these methods, however, is often adopted.

The usual method is to bend round and weld a ring

of metal upon a bar, whose diameter equals that of the
bolt. The details are as follows :—The heads are
prepared as rings (Fig. 156) cut off from a rectangular
bar of iron, and bent round upon the anvil beak or upon
a mandrel, but not welded as yet. For the shanks,

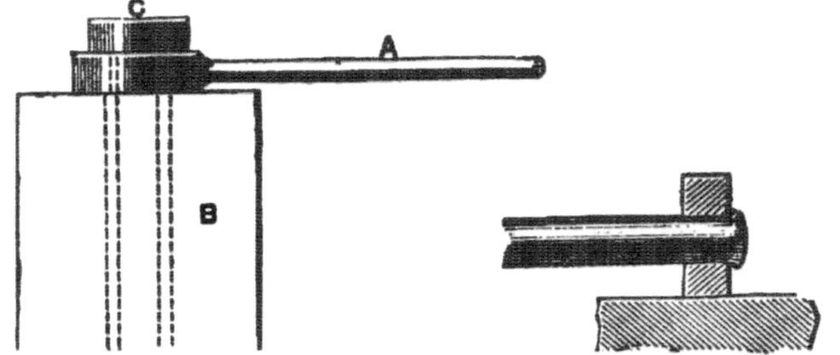

Fig. 159.—Bolt Header and
Block.

Fig. 158.—Rod burred in.

suitable lengths of round rod are cut off. To economise
time, as many rings and lengths of rod are prepared as
there are bolts wanted, and then the welding begins.
First the end of a rod, made red hot, is driven through
its ring (Fig. 157), which lies upon the anvil ; the rod is

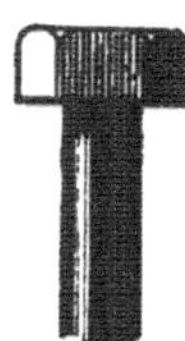

Fig. 160.—Finished Bolt
Head.

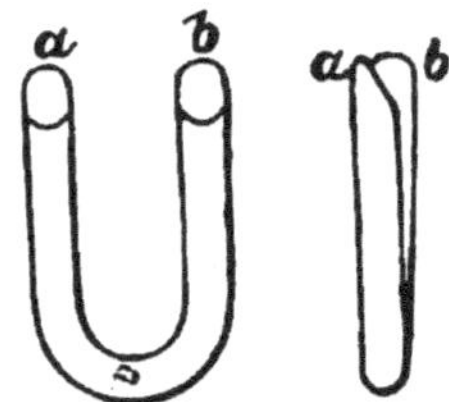

Fig. 161.—Rod Bent to Form
Chain Link.

next brought into a horizontal position, and the ring
closed tightly upon it by two or three smart blows of the
hammer, and also the end of the rod is slightly burred
over with the hammer (Fig. 158) to keep the ring from
slipping. That end is then put into the fire and raised
to a welding heat, and sand is sprinkled over it just before
withdrawal from the fire. The head is laid in a hexa-

gonal bottom tool (Fig. 60, p. 42), and about half a dozen blows given to it, altering the position of the head after each blow. It is then put into a bolt header A (Fig. 159), resting on a cast iron heading block B, pierced with a central hole, and the top of the bolt head, C, is well beaten over with hammer and flatter. The bolt is then put back in the hexagonal bottom tool (Fig. 61, p. 42)

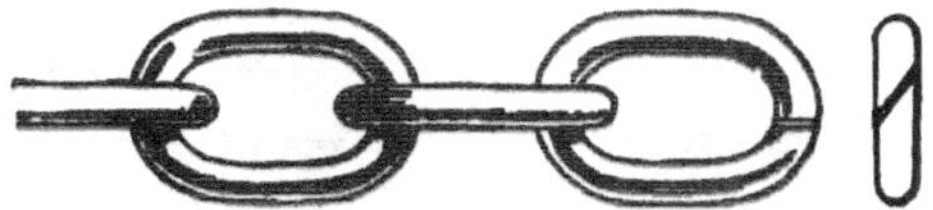

Fig. 162.—Chain Link.

and once more hammered on each separate face ; then back in the bolt header, and struck twice or thrice with a flatter, and then finished with a cup tool, which gives the rounding at the edges. Finally, it is put back in the hexagonal swage, and a last blow given with the flatter on each face. All this is done at a single heat, and, when finished (Fig. 160), the bolt head, unless very small, is still at a good red heat. A description of

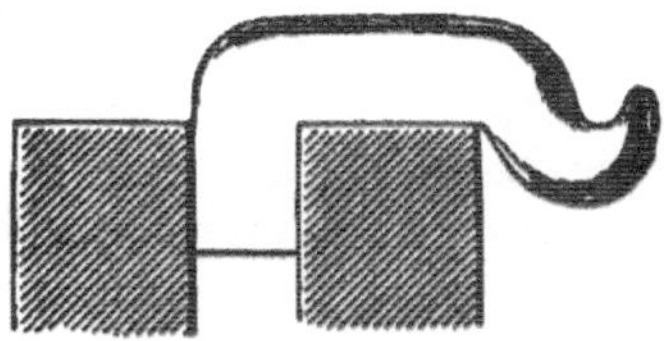

Fig. 163.—Link-forming Tool in Anvil.

an appliance used in rounding bolt heads commences on p. 18.

Many bolts, such as those used for glands and for some forms of plummer blocks, are furnished with collars. These are usually welded on as rings, and finished in a die or swage of the form in Fig. 55, p. 40.

To make nuts in small quantities, take a flat iron bar of a thickness and width the same as the nuts, and mark off and nick their lengths with a cold chisel. Centre-pop the middle of each space. Heat the

H

bar and over a bolster punch all the holes through in succession. Then cut off each nut on the anvil chisel, and finish on a mandrel.

The manufacture of chains is quite a distinct branch,

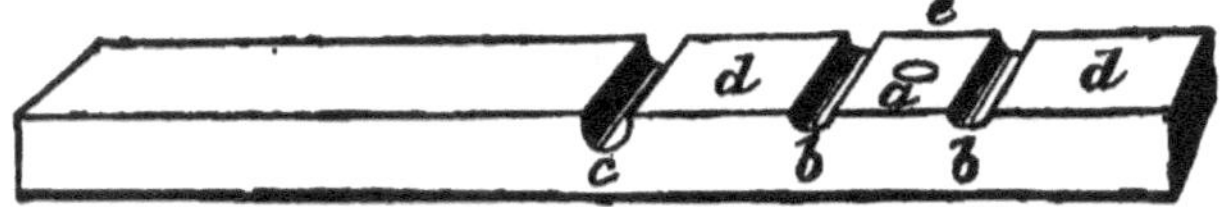

Fig. 164.—Bar Iron for Making Swivel

but a smith is often called to mend a broken chain. When a broken link is replaced it is usually made a trifle longer than the normal link, for convenience of formation. Also, when a link is added to one end of a chain

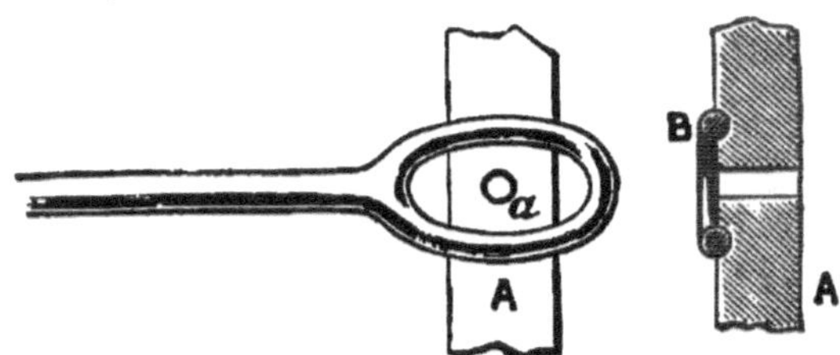

Fig. 165.—Moulding Tool for Swivel.

for the purpose of connecting it to any attachment—as a crane hook, for example—the link is made slightly longer. Such an added link is termed a shutting link.

To weld a shutting link, the iron rod is first bent to

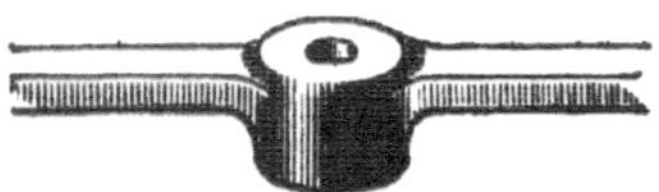

Fig. 166.—Boss of Swivel.

a U shape (Fig. 161), then two opposite faces, *a, b*, are drawn off diagonally with the hammer, and the link is bent round to bring these faces nearly close together (Fig. 162). The link is then put back into the fire and brought to a welding heat, a little sand strewn upon the joint, which is closed smartly with the hammer, first on the flat upon the anvil, and then upon a tool

(Fig. 163) fixed in the hole in the anvil. To smooth and finish the link a hollow swage tool is worked around it.

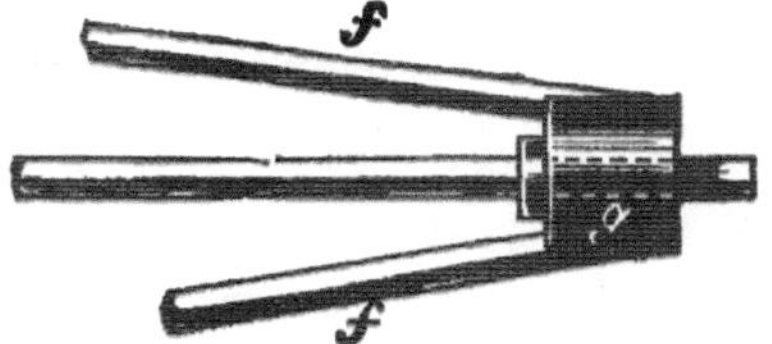

Fig. 167.—Mandrel in Swivel.

Swivels are of common occurrence, and require some art in making. Fig. 164 shows a piece of iron bar,

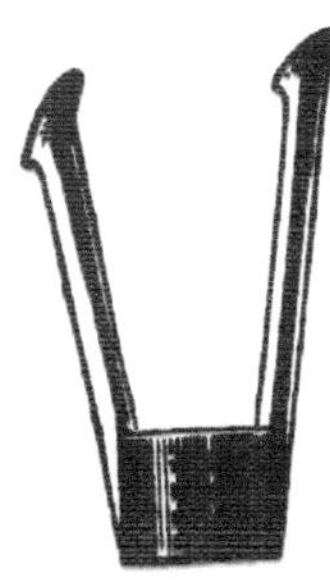

Fig. 168.—Arms of Swivel Upset for Welding.

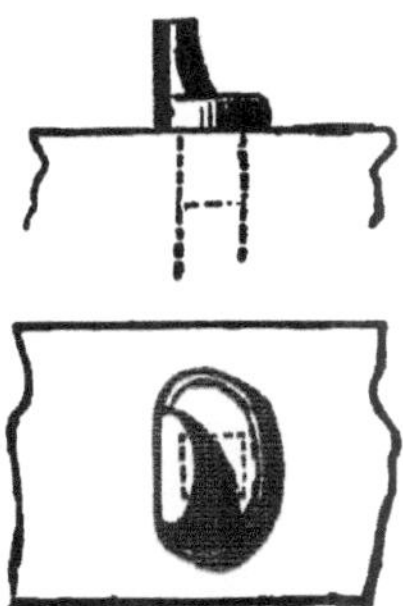

Fig. 169.—Bolster Tool for Forging Swivel.

the cross section of which should be rather greater than that of the boss of the swivel, because then neither

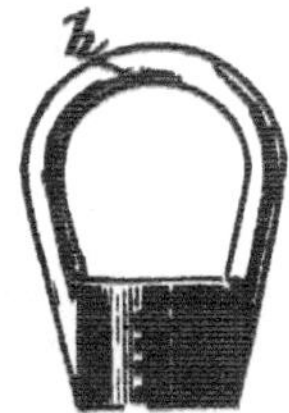

Fig. 170.—Finished Swivel.

welding on nor upsetting is necessary. A hole is first punched at *a*, corresponding with the eye of the swivel ; then a moulding tool (Fig. 165) is laid across the red-hot bar, roughly concentric with the punched hole, a, and struck a few blows with the steam hammer, leaving the impressions b, b (Fig. 164).

In the absence of a steam hammer, a fullering tool would answer the same purpose as the moulding tool, but it would take longer time. The moulding tool not only fullers, but imparts the desired curved form to the incipient boss. After fullering, the bar is cut off at c (Fig. 164), and the portions d, d, are drawn down to a

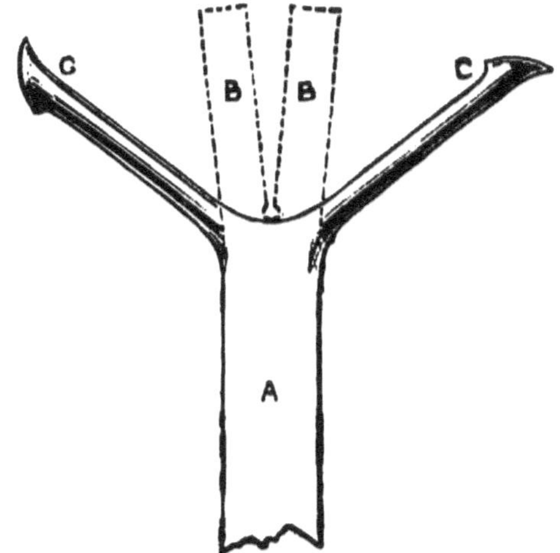

Fig. 171.—Swivel formed from Round Bar.

sectional area a trifle larger than that of the arched portions of the swivel. At the same time the boss portion is shaped out of the lump e until the forging has the appearance of Fig. 166. Then a mandrel (Fig. 167) is passed through the punched hole, a, and the drawn-down ends are hammered over as at f, f. At the same time the forging, while on the mandrel, is finished all over, except just where the weld is to be made, the boss g and the arms f, f, with their merging curves, all being gone over in detail with the hollow tools and fullers. The extreme ends of the arms f, f, are also scarfed and slightly upset, and the forging then has the appearance of Fig. 168. To afford support to the swivel during the welding, the beak of the anvil is utilised, or a special bolster-like tool (Fig. 169) is fitted into the hole in the anvil. The face of this tool is shaped roughly to the curve of the swivel, and lends itself readily to the work of welding and finishing with hollow tools, during which the position of the swivel on its bolster is being continually shifted. The form of the finished swivel is shown at Fig. 170, the scarfed weld being at h.

Another way of forming such a swivel is shown in Fig. 171. A round rod, A, is divided and forked, as seen by the dotted lines, B, the divided ends still further opened out and drawn down and upset, as at C, C ; after this, the process is similar to that previously explained.

CHAPTER VIII.

CRANKS, MODEL WORK, AND DIE FORGING.

THE blacksmith is often called upon to forge cranks and crank axles. These appear in many different forms, so it is impossible to give fully detailed accounts of the methods employed in the construction of all of them. One or two cranks of the more general kind will, therefore, be noticed.

Suppose a common bent or dip crank of round section (Fig. 172) has to be made without assistance from a die-block. It would not do simply to bend a round

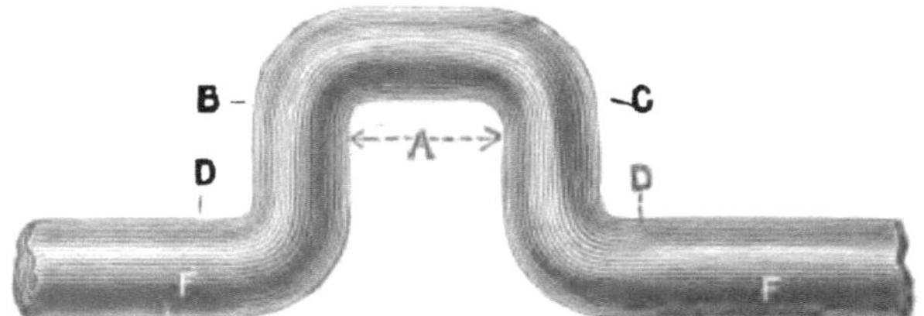

Fig. 172.—Bent Crank.

bar to the cranked form, because at the corners where the bending takes place the area would be reduced by the stretching. Bad iron is of no use for a bent crank, for the process of upsetting and bending will open out the fibres ; fagoted iron is often used.

A crank of this kind (Fig. 172) may have one, two, or three throws, and the axles extending at each end may be long or short. The cranks may be forged separately, and apart from the axles, and afterwards welded together, or all may be forged from one bar, as is most convenient.

It is supposed that the crank has only one dip ; but to a certain extent it is applicable to cranks with two or three dips, the twisting of the dips to relative angles with each other excepted.

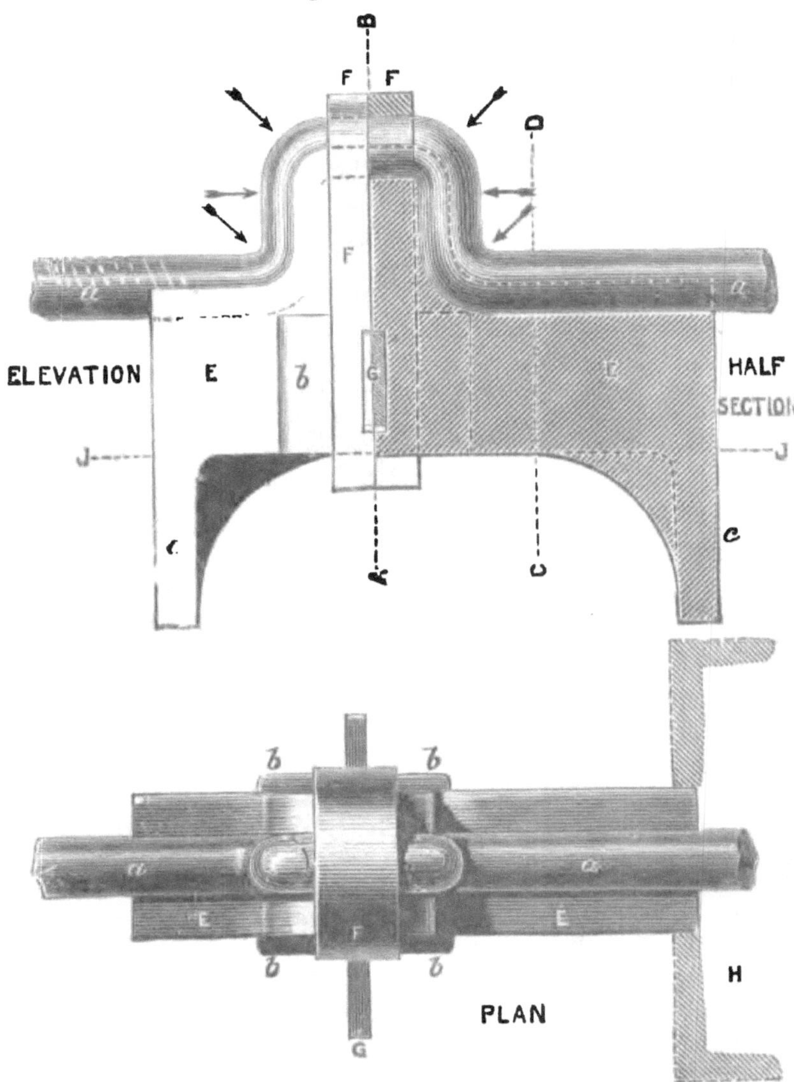

Fig. 173.—Bending Block.

Before bending the dips, there will be three upsettings of the iron : one along the length, A, that is to form the future crank pin, and the bendings, reaching from B to C in Fig. 172, where the pin merges into the webs or arms, and two others where the webs are to merge into the axle, or from B to D, and C to D (Fig. 172). These upsettings are done before the bar is bent.

The bendings at B and C will be done either at one

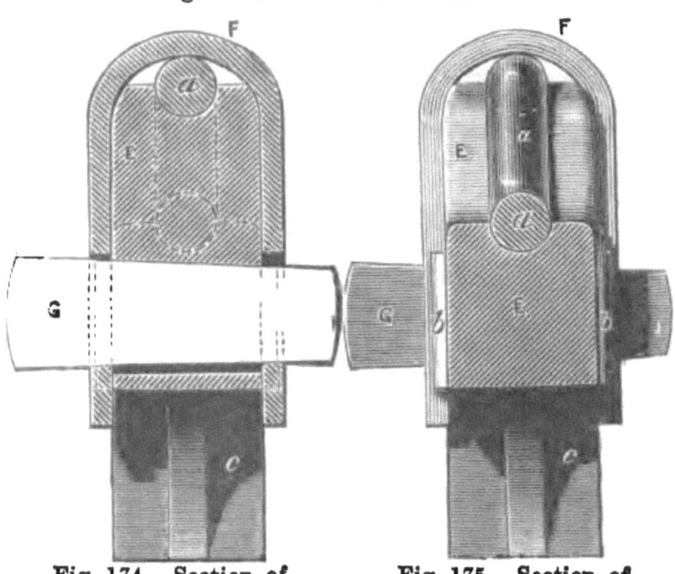

<table>
<tr><td>Fig. 174 —Section of
Bending Block.</td><td>Fig. 175.—Section of
Bending Block.</td></tr>
</table>

or two heats.   If the pin is short, one heat will suffice, but if long, two will be necessary.   Here the swage block, or the levelling block pierced with numerous holes, is of use ; a couple of pins inserted into holes in either block, form suitable supports in pulling the axles round and preserve the true plane of the dip.   If neither swage block nor levelling block is available, a pin placed in the anvil hole must answer the same purpose, but it will not be suitable for heavy work.

It is necessary to check the width, A (Fig. 172),

before bending the other corners. Upsetting must be resorted to if too great, and drawing down ·if not enough.

The bending of the corners D, E, can be done around suitable pins, the axles F, F, affording good leverage. After this the crank webs from B to D, and from C to E, must be set parallel, and the axles F, F, set for alignment lengthways, and be brought into the same plane with the webs and pin.

In· cranks of this type, it is desirable and usual to have rather an excess of metal at the corners, especially when they are to be finished bright. Such cranks, when made in quantities, are usually bent over a block, or they are stamped.

A bending block is shown in plan and elevation by Fig. 173. A section on A, B, is shown by Fig. 175, and another on C, D, by Fig. 174. The block is a casting, E, sufficiently heavy to resist the hammer blows necessary for making the bends of the crank. Its width is therefore considerably greater than the diameter of the crank, and ample depth is given. The length is sufficient to permit of true alignment of the axle being made, though not necessarily so great as that of the crank axle. The distances from the centre line A B to each end are made unequal to permit of the forging of cranks with two throws or three throws. For single dip cranks only the lengths would be equal. In Fig. 173 the right-hand end is made sufficiently long to afford a good bedding for the axle *a*, but the left-hand end is made short, so that after one throw is forged it may lie beyond the left-hand end to permit of the bending of the second or the third throw upon the block.

In the formation of a crank by the aid of such a block, those sections where the bendings are to be made are thickened by upsetting as before described, and the webs are bent upon the levelling block or upon the swage block, and the axles bent at right angles with the webs approximately true, though not necessarily so carefully as though the crank were intended to be finished by this method. The advantage of the block now becomes apparent. The crank *a*, heated nearly to a welding heat, is dropped over the block E, embraced by the strap F, tightened by the cottar C, which being driven in rapidly holds it in place, and the webs and the axles are bedded down into the curved recess of the block, hammer, fuller, and hollow tools being quickly brought into requisition wherever wanted. Thus the crank is

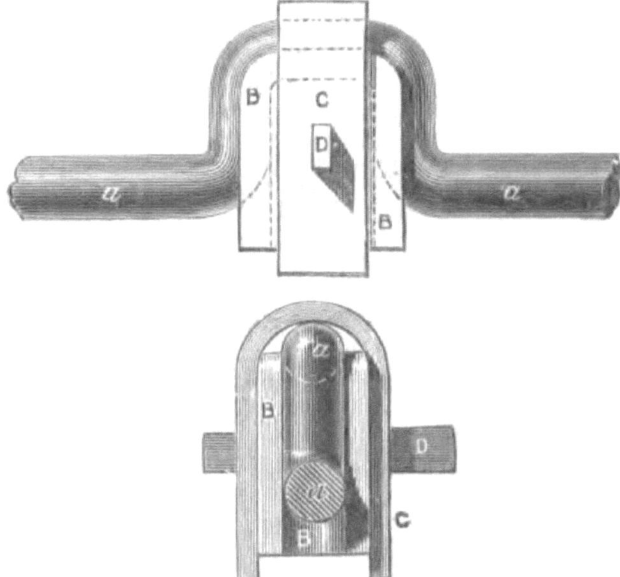

Fig. 176.—Filling-in Block.

practically finished, only a little smoothing over being done after removal from the block, chiefly at the sides which cannot be got at while the crank lies on·the block. The crank should be removed from the block soon, or it will become bound tight, owing to the shrinkage of the metal by cooling. For this reason the sides of the block should be tapered slightly, and for large cranks, when making the block, allowance for shrinkage in cooling should be given at the rate of about $\frac{1}{4}$ in. per foot.

In Fig. 173, *b*, *b*, are guide strips cast upon the sides of the block E for the strap F. If the strap is not sufficiently stout, a clamp or a rough gib may hold its bottom ends together. The two horns, C, C, are cast on for convenience. As the blows for the most part are delivered in the direction of the arrows, the block needs to be steadied endwise ; therefore, in the example from which this is taken, a heavy cast-iron block is sunk into the ground, a little below the shop floor. It is grooved out at one end to take the parts *c*, *c*, which preserve the bending block steady under the hammer blows. The grooved end of this casting is shown dotted at H, Fig. 173 ; *c*, *c*, are below the ground—J J being the level of the floor.

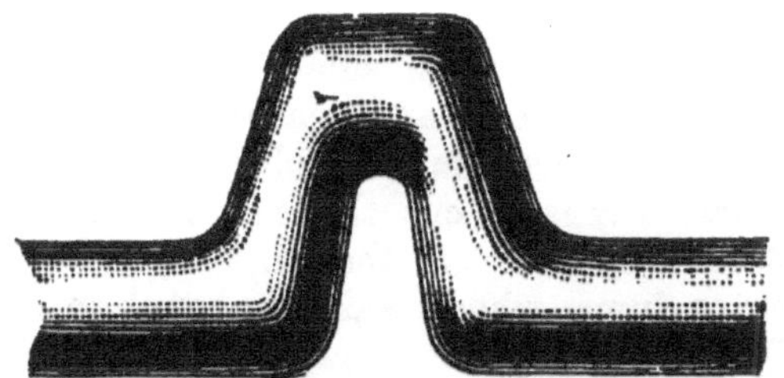

Fig. 177.—Crank roughly fullered into form

If a second or third dip has to be forged, the truth of the first one is preserved by inserting in the dip a packing block B, Fig. 176, which gives an elevation and side view. This is a cast-iron piece hollowed semi-circularly to fit the webs, and secured in place with a strap, C, and cottar, D. This is retained in place until the remaining dip or dips are bent. Fig. 177 shows a form of crank axle that is well adapted for forging into the strongest form possible, the fibre running round the bent portions. In some other forms the same advantageous disposition of metal is not secured.

Formerly it was quite common to see the largest crank axles of the general form shown in Fig. 178 built up by preparing separately the pin A, the webs B, and the axles C, and welding them together. The webs were opened out at the one end to embrace the pin and at the other end to embrace the axle, and then all welded together. Now it is usual in very large cranks, on marine engines especially, to make and machine each of these parts separately and weld them together, shrinking

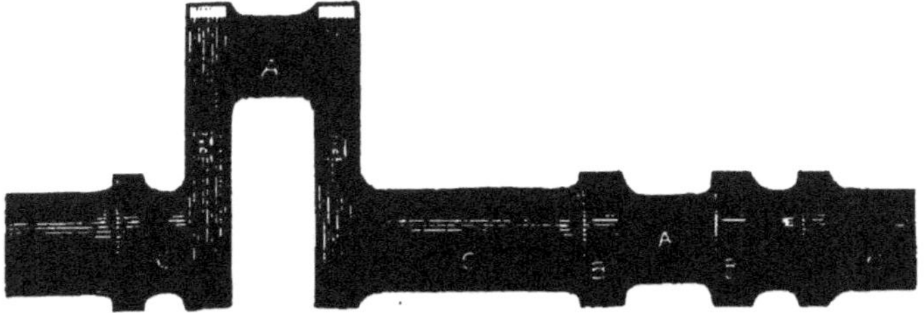

Fig. 178.—Locomotive Type of Crank.

the webs on to the pin. In small cranks of this type the forging is made solid and machined out. Briefly, the methods employed are as follows :—The simplest and the worst way is to cut the entire crank out of a slab. Better than this is the drawing down of the axles from a lump whose width is equal to the total

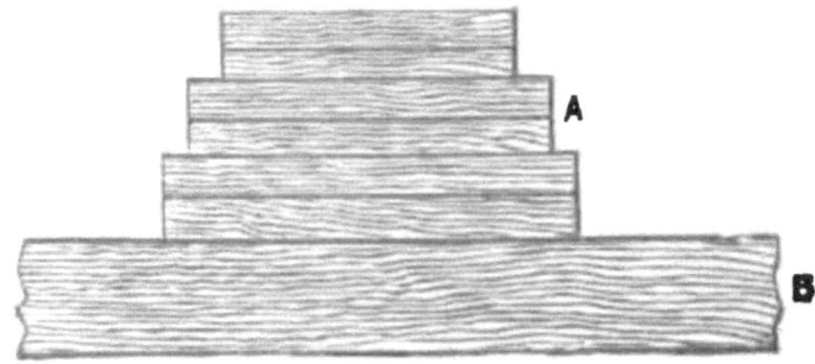

Fig. 179.—Piled Crank Lump.

width of the crank from the outer edge of the axle to the outer edge of the pin. Better still is the fullering out of a lump in such a way that an approximately curved disposition of the fibres is obtained (see Fig. 177), leaving, however, a good deal of finishing and machining to be done afterwards.

Another way—not so good as the last, but more common—is to weld on one or several pieces, A, to

one side of the bar, B, that is to form the axle
(Fig. 179), leaving the gap to be slotted out or drilled
out.

In cranks having two and three throws, the gaps
stand at angles of 90° and .120° respectively.   Cranks
like Fig. 172 are usually forged with the dips at proper
angles, but those like Fig. 180 are more often forged with
the dips in one plane and twisted afterwards.   When
built, they are sometimes forged approximately at these
angles.   Sometimes each crank is prepared separately,
and welded to suitable lengths of axle.   When twisting
is practised it must be performed over as great a length
of shaft as possible, in order to be gradual.   Two or
three heats may have to be given if the length is

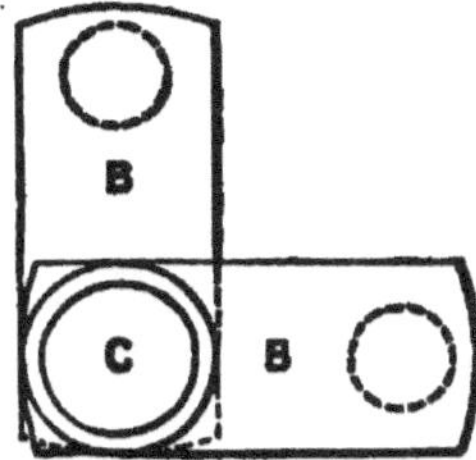

Fig. 180.—Locomotive Type of Crank.

considerable, and a portion of the necessary twist imparted at each heat.   One crank will have to be
secured by some means, such as clamping down to the
swage or levelling block or anvil, or holding under the
steam hammer, or in the vice, while leverage is exerted
at the other end.   The leverage may be applied direct
to the other crank, or to the axle itself, by means of
clips.   A few well-directed blows of the hammer will
assist and serve to regulate the dead pull exerted upon
the lever.   If the cranks are welded to the axle, a long
and somewhat bulky scarf should be made, to give
plenty of metal for subsequent consolidation and swaging
down.

The bosses for some large stationary engine-cranks
when they are not upset, or the webs not swaged from

the solid, are built up or bent round in various fashions. In one method the boss is formed by bending round a piece of bar *a*, and welding it to a straight portion B (Fig. 181). The bending is usually done by placing the bar across two supports, and fullering it down at the central portion. When the bar is thus partly bent, the curving is finished by closing the ends

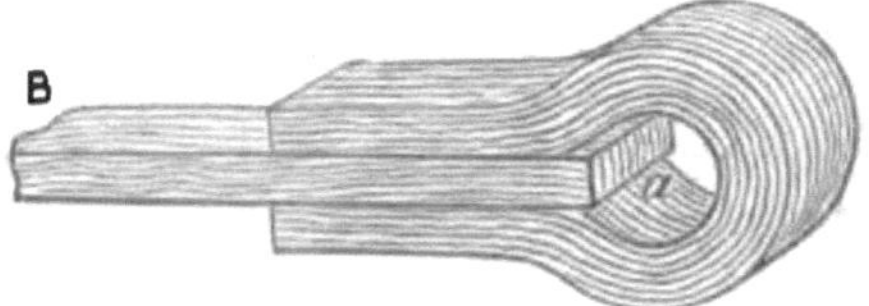

Fig. 181.—Crank Boss.

upon the anvil, till they just embrace the flat bar B in readiness for welding ; more than one thickness of metal may be employed in the formation of the boss.

To finish such a boss, any excess of metal at the end, *a*, of the bar is cut off with a chisel, a mandrel is then inserted in the hole, and the outer curves finished with fullers.

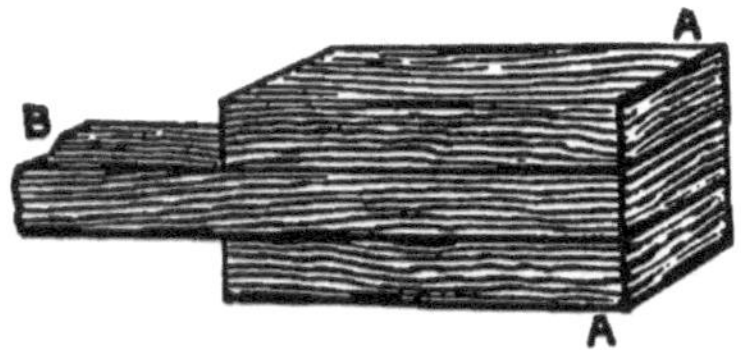

Fig. 182.—Lump for Crank Boss.

Often, however, the boss is made simply by piling (Fig. 182). The pieces A, A, of any convenient thickness, are welded to the straight bar B, and afterwards are consolidated at a welding heat ; a rudely curved form is imparted to them by means of fullering tools before final shaping with the set and finishing tools.

When the two bosses are prepared, the ends B, which have served as porters, are cut off, and the bosses united by means of a scarfed joint, thus forming a double-ended boss whose middle portion, or web, can be fullered and swaged down to the lesser section required.

When extra strong and sound forgings are wanted, a solid new bar is not used, but a large number of selected pieces of any size and shape are welded together, the operation being known as piling or fagoting. The pieces are laid together in bundles of suitable sizes, bound round with iron to a porter or long bar of iron, and heated and welded and reduced under the steam hammer. For special work this process is repeated two or three times, the pile being drawn down, and then cut off into lengths that are re-piled, and re-heated, and welded. The bars are not merely laid in parallel series, but are often made to cross one another at various angles, to secure greater strength. By this means, not only are forgings with the maximum of strength procurable, but all the odds and ends of metal cut off in the processes of forging are utilised.

Forgings for model work are necessarily expensive. In the first place, in order to produce shapely and accurate forgings, much time must be spent upon them. In the second place, very few smiths care to undertake such work, because ordinary forging pays better, and because a man must execute very neat work to turn out perfect model forgings. Yet it is work that practised amateurs, with time at their disposal, can succeed fairly well with, because patience more than high skill is wanted, and scarcely any of the really difficult operations of forgings are involved. Few special tools are required, most of the work being done with hammers and files. The cost of material is small, and the principal appliances are a small anvil and a vice.

In touching upon the differences between model and general work, it may be said generally that there is less of welding and more of drawing down done in forgings for model work than in those of heavy type. The difference in the dimensions of bossed-up ends or forked ends and their shanks or rods is so small relatively, that it is much easier to reduce the rods with the hammer than to weld the ends on. There is no great difficulty in welding small work, provided no time is lost in hammering the parts together immediately on removal from the fire.

For very light work, a small combined anvil and vice will probably be found serviceable. One advantage of a small anvil is that the beak is very useful to bend curves, and to form a suitable bedding when fullering down curved necks and shoulders for which the ordinary fullering tools are too large. The cross peens of the hammers are useful for this operation, and with different sizes various curvatures can be formed. Flatters are not used, all the battering and smoothing that is done being effected with the hand hammer.

Owing to the unsuitability of smiths' ordinary finishing tools for purposes of model work, the file has to be used much more largely in this class of work than in ordinary forgings. When the forgings are cooling down to a black heat, a good deal of material can be removed with little effort, and a certain amount of finish imparted.

Again, in small forged work, many parts are left solid that in large work would be punched or fullered or cut out. The holes in bosses would seldom be punched, but wholly drilled. The forked ends of eccentric rods are left to be slotted or filed out.

In wrought iron used for model forgings, the same regard must be had to the direction of the grain as in larger forgings. But, in all respects steel is preferable as a material for model work to wrought iron. It is hard, rigid, and strong—important considerations—takes a better polish, and is more durable.

Die forging, or stamping, is adopted by the smith for repetition work. There are numerous parts in nearly all branches of smiths' work that are required precisely alike, and an enormous saving is effected by the use of dies. Such parts as flat links for chain, flanges for steam and exhaust pipes, some portions of valve gear, ornamental bosses, railing heads, pins, small levers, and similar articles more or less intricate, can be readily stamped with proper appliances.

Large dies are usually made of cast iron, and the smaller of steel. In large dies the required impressions are cast, and afterwards cleaned and smoothed a little with the file ; in small dies they have to be cut out with drills, chisels, and files. In either case, sufficient metal must be put into the die to enable it to withstand the concussion of the blows. Cast dies are frequently bonded with a wrought-iron ring, in order to prevent their bursting. For this kind of work the sledge is of no use, generally the drop hammer, steam hammer, or hydraulic press being used. In little shops unprovided with power, the Oliver often serves.

In the plainest work a single die will often suffice, and the formation of the die must vary with the shapes of the forgings. But if the top of a forging is not flat, then two dies must be used, the upper portion being cut to the requisite outline. The top portion must also be attached to the lower in such a way that it will take its proper position in relation to the lower instantly, without any adjustment. This is usually effected by means of iron dowels, two or three dowels being driven tightly into the lower portion of the die, and standing upwards to fit loosely into corresponding holes drilled in the top portion of the die. The dowels are well tapered, and their ends rounded off so as to go more easily into the holes in the top portion of the die. The bottom dies are sometimes furnished with long handles, or they are lifted about with the hoop tongs, the top dies alone being furnished with handles. When holes have to be punched in the forgings, corresponding holes are usually drilled in top and bottom dies. The top holes are then parallel, and of the same size as the punch which is inserted in them ; but the bottom ones are of the same size only where the lower face of the forging lies, being

I

tapered downwards to allow the punched discs to fall through freely.

In many cases two sets of dies are requisite to produce an article ; one set will form the sides, and another set the top and bottom. Of course, dies are expensive and, as a general rule, only pay when there are at least several dozens of an article required.

In stamped work, the amount of material required for any given forging must be gauged with accuracy. If there is an excess of metal, there will be thick fins spreading over the edges. If, on the other hand, the metal is short, then the forgings will not come up keen and clean, but will have edges more or less rounding and inaccurate.

CHAPTER IX.

HOME-MADE PORTABLE FORGES.

ILLUSTRATIONS and brief descriptions of some of the better known forges are given in Chapter I., but it is

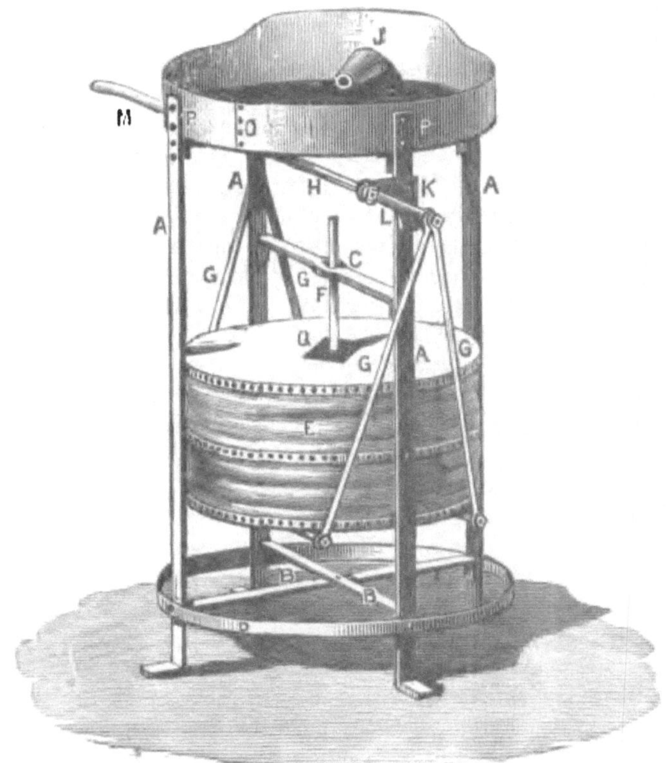

Fig. 183.—Home-made Portable Forge.

thought that some readers, instead of buying a forge ready-made, may wish to construct one themselves. Such readers will be interested in the following particulars of a portable forge which can be easily made by an iron-worker. The appliance (Fig. 183) consists of a wrought-iron frame, on the top of which is the tray, or hearth ; and underneath is the bellows and blowing arrangement.

The whole of the framework is made of 1 in. by ⅜ in. square iron bar, and is riveted together by ⅜ in. by ⅞ in. and ⅜ in. by 1¼ in. iron rivets, the holes being bored to allow the rivets to fit in rather right. The dimensions of the various parts of the framework are all in the illustrations.

The framework consists of four legs A,A,A,A (Fig. 183), braced together by the cross-stays, B, B, two above and two below the bellows. The two stays above the bellows are not shown in the figure, being hidden by the tray, etc. They are of the same form and dimensions as the bottom pair, except at the centre, where they cross each other, one of them being cranked down to allow the other to cross at its own level, and thus make a level bed for the hearth-tray to rest on. One of the legs is shown in front and side elevation in Fig. 184.

The various parts of the framework should first be forged and cut to dimensions given in drawings, and tried to make sure that they are all exact before marking out for drilling. The two cross-stays, B, B (Fig. 183), are riveted together where they cross in the centre of the frame as shown. The ring, D (Fig. 183), is placed round the outside of frame at the points where the cross-stays are riveted to the legs, and the rivets pass through the ring, D, legs, A, A, A, A, and cross-stays, B, B, binding them all securely together.

The hearth consists of a flat, round plate of iron, sufficiently thick to withstand the heat ; it is more serviceable, though a little more expensive, if made of thinner material and a circular fireclay brick bottom is placed on it. The hearth-plate rests on the top pair of cross-stays, and is riveted to them by four rivets, two in each stay. The circular band, I, surrounding the hearth is cut out of ₁⁶₆ in. sheet iron to the shape shown at

Fig. 185; the hole A is for the introduction of the tuyere,

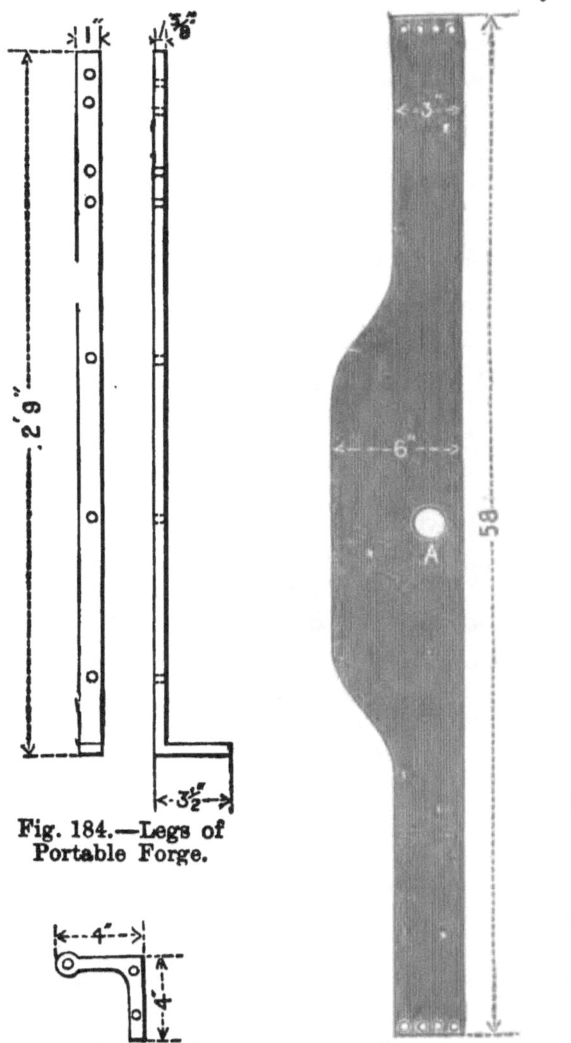

Fig. 184.—Legs of Portable Forge.

Fig. 186.—Bracket for Supporting Lever of Portable Forge.

Fig. 185. — Pattern for Portable Forge Tray.

J, from the bellows.   The band is riveted to the top of

each leg by two rivets, as shown at P, P (Fig. 183), and is also riveted together at its two ends, as shown at o, by four rivets.   The hearth - plate is cut to exactly fit inside the band, I, and to rest on the top pair of cross-stays.

The bellows work consists of a spindle of ⅜-in. round iron, working in two brackets, shown at K (Fig. 183), and in detail by Fig. 186.   One of these brackets is riveted

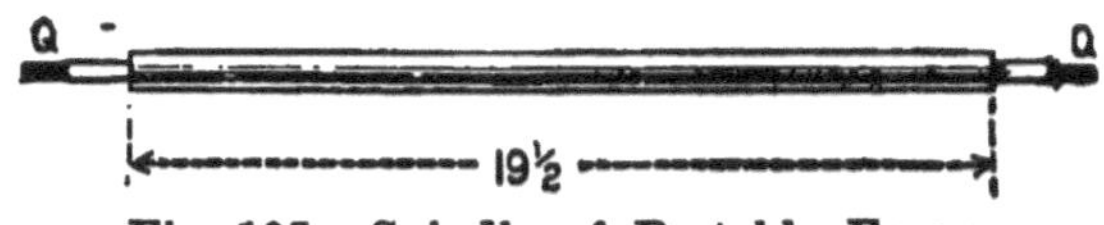

Fig. 187.—Spindle of Portable Forge.

to each of two opposite legs, by two rivets in each as shown in Fig. 183.   The spindle is shown at H (Fig. 183), and also by Fig. 187, the ends, Q, being squared (see Fig. 188) to fit the small cranks, L, and the long lever, M (Fig. 183).   These cranks are shown in plan and elevation in Fig. 189, and the long lever in Fig. 190.   As will be seen from Fig. 188, the ends of the lever are squared and screwed.   The length for the square part is ¾ in.   This is for the end carrying the long lever, as well as the crank ;

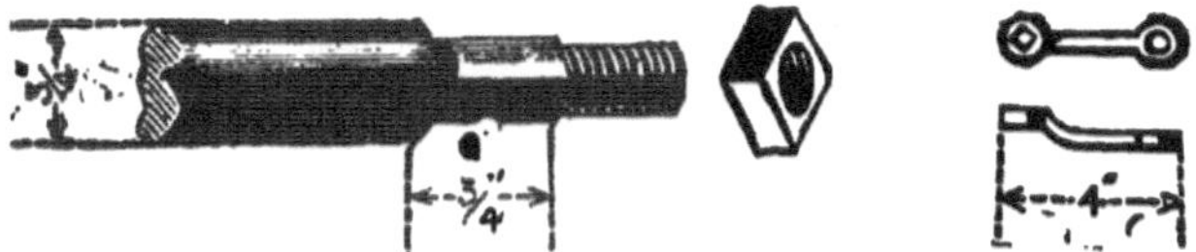

Fig. 188.—End of Spindle of Portable Forge.

Fig. 189.—Crank on
End of Spindle of
Portable Forge.

the otner end, which carries only a crank, will have the squared part ½ in. long.

The cross-stay, c (Fig. 183), acts as a guide to ensure the top chamber of the bellows rising and falling per-pendicularly.   It is secured to one pair of legs by rivets as the cross-stays are ; it is made of 1 in. by ¾ in. iron bar, swelled out and has a hole in the centre, as shown at Fig. 191, to allow the guide-rod, F (Fig. 183), to slide easily through.   The upright ½-in. round guide-rod and square plate are shown in Fig. 192. The plate is countersunk to receive four screws, which attach it to the top board of the bellows, the rod being riveted into the plate. The bellows, E (Fig. 183), is fastened to the frame by four stout wood screws, one through each leg. Between the legs and the centre board of bellows are placed four pieces of ½-in. iron pipe, each about 1 in. long; the four screws pass through the legs into these

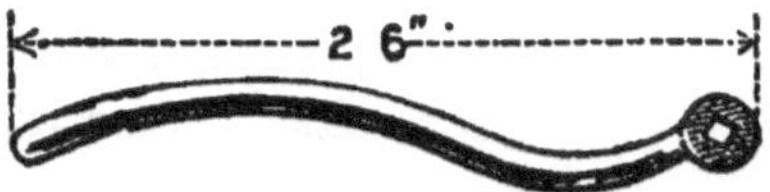

Fig. 190.—Lever on End of Spindle of Portable Forge.

pieces of pipe, and are driven home into the centreboard of bellows, holding them quite securely.

The bottom chamber of the bellows is supported by four links, shown at G, G, G, G (Fig. 183). Each end of these links is swelled out (see Fig. 193) at the bottom ends, and has a hole to fit on the round ends of two flat bars made of 1 in. by ⅜ in. iron bar, running across the bottom board of bellows (shown in Fig. 194), and at the top ends for the reception of the ⅜-in. bolts, which

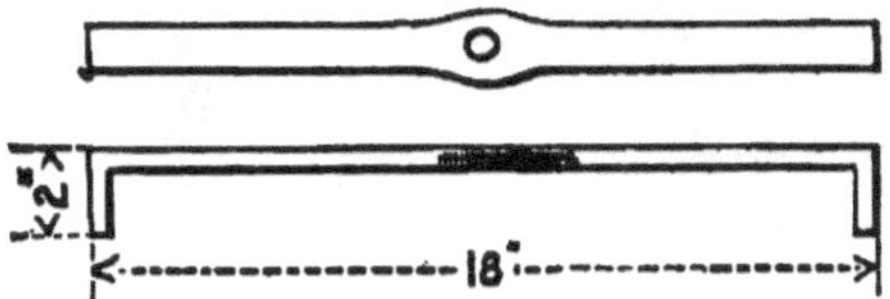

Fig. 191.—Guide-stay for Bellows of Portable Forge.

connect them to the short crank, L (Fig. 183). This arrangement is better seen at Fig. 195, L being the short crank, G, G the links, and Z the ⅜-in. bolt and nut. The flat bars just mentioned are drawn out to a round section at the ends, and screwed for nuts, which keep the links in their place. They are fastened to the bottom board of the bellows by three screws in each passing through holes drilled and countersunk to receive them.

The bellows is composed of three circular boards of

inch stuff, 14½ in. in diameter.   The middle and bottom boards are each provided with a valve, opening upwards.   These are made by drilling a hole, 2 in. in

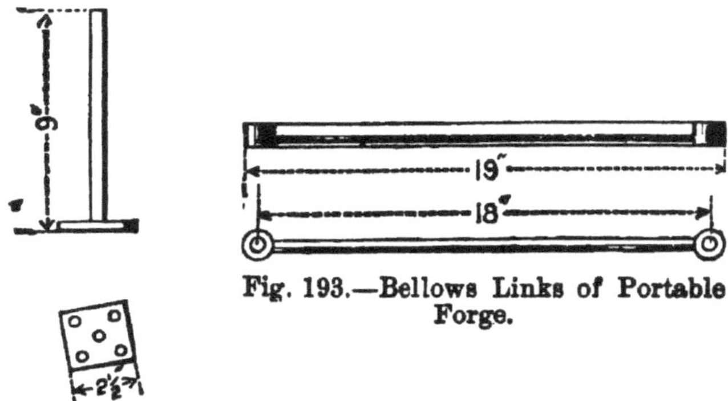

Fig. 193.—Bellows Links of Portable Forge.

Fig. 192.—Guide-pin for Portable Forge Bellows.

diameter, in the centre of each board.   Over each of these holes is placed a flat, circular piece of leather nailed to the board at one side which forms a hinge,

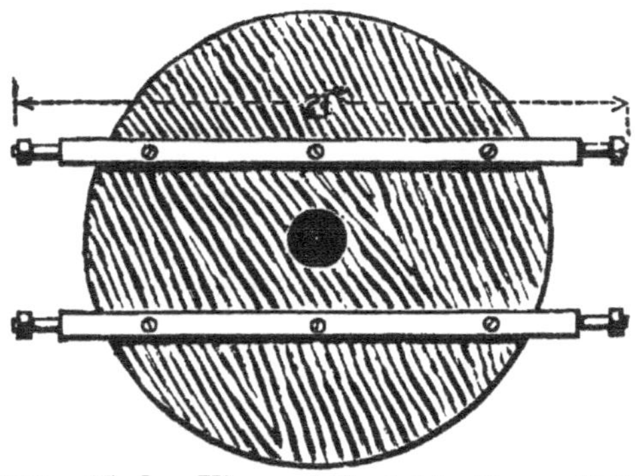

Fig. 194.—Under View of Portable Forge Bellows.

but otherwise free to move up and down for the passage of the air.   A piece of wood is glued on the top of the leathers, to ensure that they shall drop flat and close the valve when the air is within.

A wire stop, s (Fig. 196), is driven into the board, to

prevent the wood valves turning completely over, in which case they would not again close when required. The middle board has a block of wood fastened to it, for the reception of the screwed end of the pipe conveying the blast from the bellows to the hearth.

The three boards are fastened together by a piece of leather 14 in. wide, which goes all round them, and is securely nailed to their edges by 1-in. clout nails, placed in two rows, and as near together as possible. The leather of the bellows covering should be of good quality, and may be obtained at any leather-seller's. It is scarcely likely that a piece will be obtained suffi-

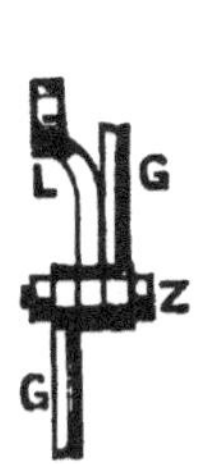

Fig. 195. — Link and Crank Connection of Portable Forge.

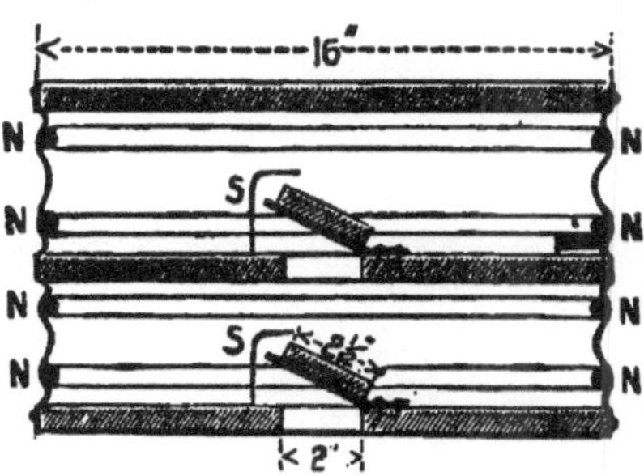

Fig. 196.—Section through Portable Forge Bellows.

ciently large to make it entire, so it may have to be joined. A strip of leather, 1 in. in width, is placed round the edge of each board over the leather covering, and the clout nails are driven through this and the leather covering into the boards. Before fixing the leather on to the boards, two rings of ¼-in. round iron bar, 14½ in. diameter outside, are inserted in each chamber. These are to keep the leather stretched outward, and to ensure it forming even creases when opening and closing. The two ends of the circular band of leather covering the bellows should be joined with copper rivets and washers, such as are used in leather hose, put as near together as possible.

The pipe leading the air blast from the bellows to the

hearth is of ¾-in. iron tube, and is shown in section, with its fittings, by Fig. 197. At the bottom it is screwed into the wood block T, and at the top into the tuyere, J, through the iron band encircling the hearth, with a back nut and washer to keep it secure. The tuyere should be of thick wrought iron, and tapped to receive the end of the ¾-in. tube as shown. The forge is now complete, and it only remains to regulate the flow of air by putting weights on the top board of bellows.

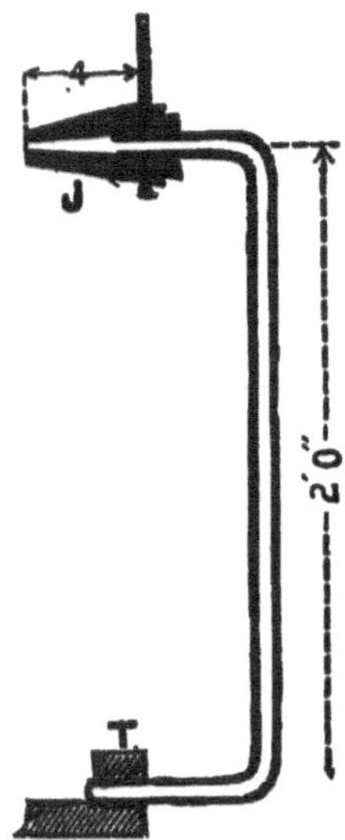

Fig. 197.—Nozzle and Bellows Connection of Portable Forge.

Weights should also be suspended from the bottom board sufficient to draw the lever up when pressed down.

Of course, the dimensions of the forge may be varied, and the material can even be made lighter; but, owing to the knocking about such a forge has to sustain, it will be best to keep as near as possible to the dimensions given.

Another portable forge (Fig. 198) is made of wrought iron, with the exception of the tuyere; this may be the hub of a plough or other wheel. The legs (A, Fig. 198)

are of 1-in. angle iron 1 ft. 6 in. long. The sides and end-
plates are of 4½-in. by ½-in. fender plate, and are respectively 18 in. and 15 in. long. One of the end-plates is

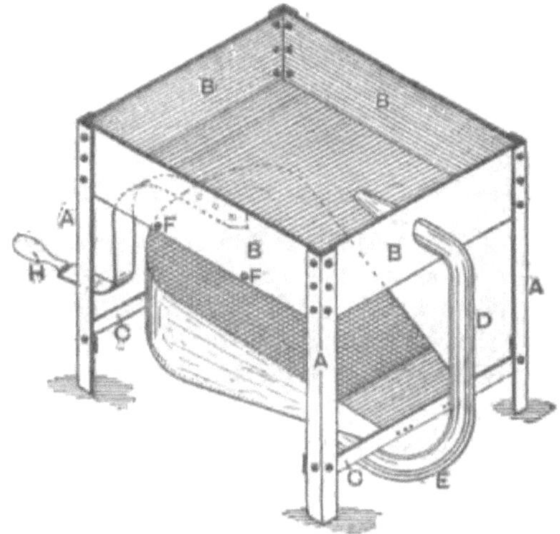

Fig. 198.—Small Portable Forge.

drilled through with a 1¼-in. hole for the reception of
the blast-pipe D (Fig. 198). C, C are the stays as set out
in Fig. 199 ; they strengthen the legs and support the

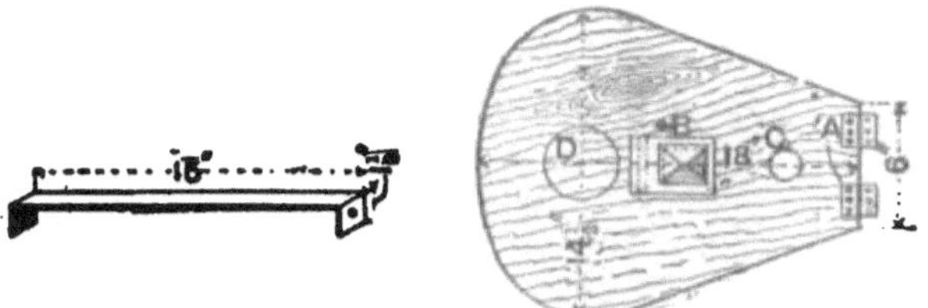

Fig. 199.—Stay of Portable   Fig. 200.—Plan of Portable
        Forge.   Forge Bellows.

bellows. The single-blast bellows, as shown in detail
by Fig. 200, are made of two 1-in. pine boards, cut to
the dimensions given, and hinged by cast butts at A ; B
is the valve which is required in one board only ; C is
the hole for the delivery-pipe ; the bend with union

shown at E (Fig. 198) and D (Fig. 200) indicates the position of the bellows spiral spring. The bellows, which is made of basil leather, opens to 7½ in. H (Fig. 198) may be either a handle or a step, or a combination of

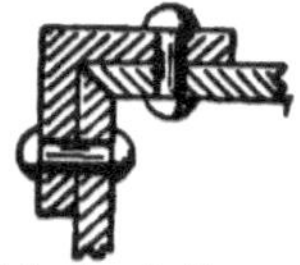

Fig. 201.—Joint of Corner of Hearth.

both. F, F (Fig. 198) show the rivets which hold a ledge inside to support the bottom of the forge. This bottom is of soft steel, 18 in. by 15 in. The delivery-pipe is threaded at G (Fig. 198) for 4 in., and a nut (not shown) on each side of the fender plate holds it securely

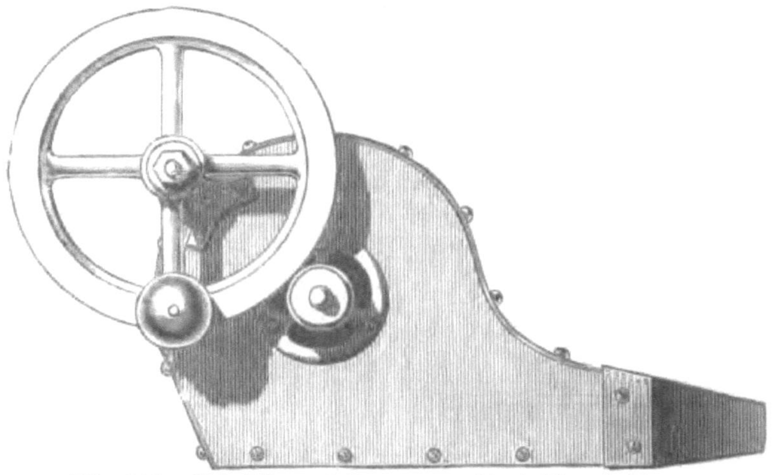

Fig. 202.—Side View of Continuous-blast Blow-bellows.

in its place. The bellows is secured by ordinary screws, which pass through the stays, but small bolts might be used with advantage. The whole thing is fixed together with round-headed rivets ½ in. by $\frac{3}{16}$ in.; the sides may be filed to a mitre joint, see Fig. 201.

The construction of a continuous blast blow-bellows

(see Figs. 202 and 203) will now be dealt with. These emit a continuous current of air instead of the intermittent current of the old - fashioned ones; instead of getting the draught from a $\frac{3}{16}$-in. hole, or thereabouts, it is got through a hole $2\frac{1}{2}$ in. wide and $\frac{3}{4}$ in. deep, and these bellows cost only about half as much.

To commence the construction of the bellows, cut out the sides and the bottom, but do not screw them together.

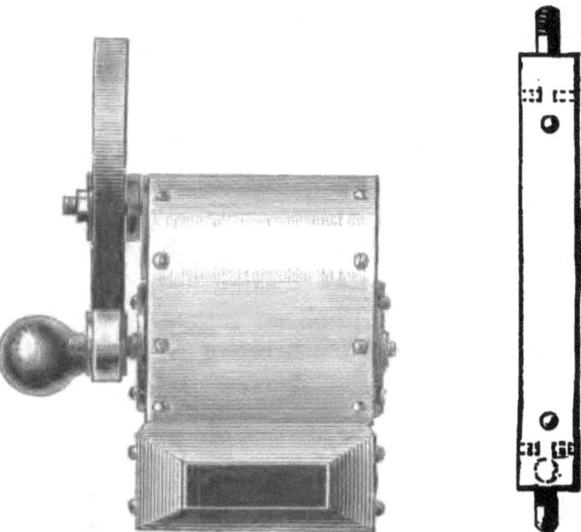

Fig. 203.—Front View of Continuous-blast Blow-bellows.

Fig. 204.—Spindle of Blow-bellows.

Make a spindle (as Figs. 204 and 205), drill two holes in each side, one at each end, as shown, and tap them and screw a piece of wire to fit; cut it into pieces about $\frac{3}{16}$ in. long, and screw a piece into each hole. Four pieces of tin, a little narrower than the bellows, have corresponding holes punched in them for the pieces of wire to slip through; put one of them on, slip a washer over the wire, and then rivet it over. Treat all in the same way, and then screw the brass bearings (Fig. 206) to the sides, fit in the iron spindle, and screw sides and bottom together, afterwards screwing the piece of metal over the top.

The wheel will have to be bought. Fig. 207 is a sketch of spindle for it to run on. Turn this up, screw

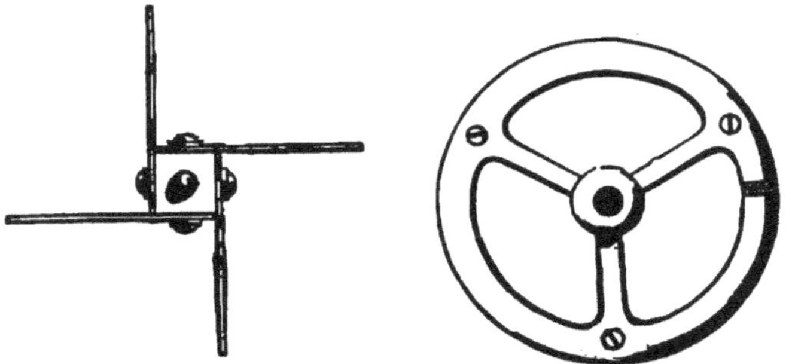

Fig. 205.—Side View of Blow-bellows Spindle.

Fig. 206.—Brass Bearing for Sides of Blow-bellows.

it at each end, fix it with a nut to the plate (Fig. 208), put on the wheel, and keep it there by a washer and another nut, then fit the knob on rather loosely. But before fixing the wheel, turn a bit of wood (Fig. 209)

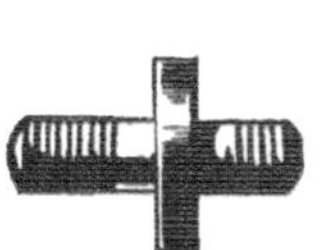

Fig. 207.—Brass Spindle for Blow-bellows Wheel.

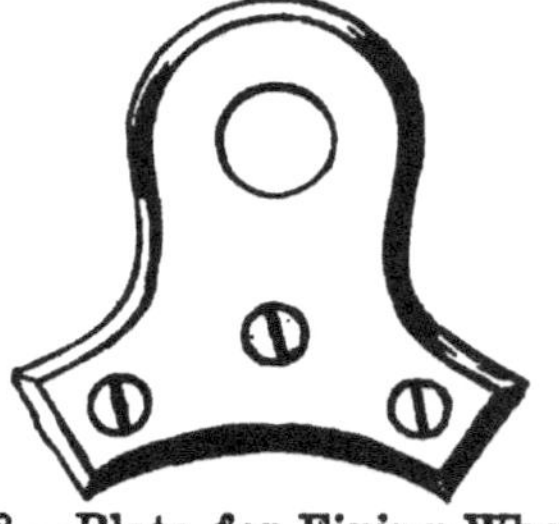

Fig. 208.—Plate for Fixing Wheel of Spindle.

and over it put an indiarubber band, and screw this on to the projecting end of the iron spindle ; fix the wheel against this tightly. In Fig. 210 is shown the shape of the nose-piece. When correctly cut out, bend this over at right angles at all the dotted lines, and it will fit on the end of the bellows. Either rivet or solder together the two edges, A and B, then drill it and screw it on.

When this is all done, turn the handle rapidly; the fan inside will then revolve at a good rate, and a strong draught will be obtained. Of course, the fan can have five or even six wings, but in such a case it is advisable

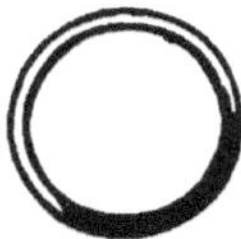 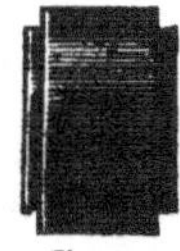

Fig. 209.—Wood to Screw on Spindle of Blower.

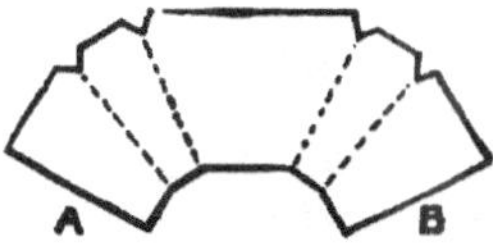

Fig. 210.—Pattern for Nozzle of Blower.

to strengthen the wings by soldering pieces of wire between them, as in Fig. 211.

Another improvement is to turn a small groove in the iron wheel, and fix it a little further away from the iron spindle; turn up a smaller wheel, put a groove

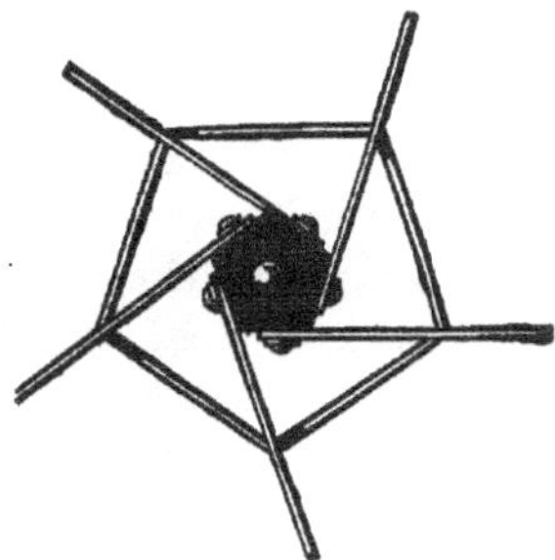

Fig. 211.—Side View of Blow-bellows Spindle and Fan.

in it also, and screw it on to the end of the iron spindle; it could then be run with a band. It works very well, however, with the wheel fixed against an indiarubber-covered knob, as previously explained.

It is preferable to substitute gun-metal for the brass in all parts except the covering and nose-piece.

CHAPTER X.

MANIPULATING STEEL AT THE FORGE.

FROM the foregoing chapters it will have been seen that pure metallic iron has but little commercial use, and, in fact, in this state is comparatively unknown; it is when combined with carbon, sometimes modified by other elements, that pure iron becomes the iron of commerce, and is known as malleable iron, steel, and cast iron, as the proportion of carbon is increased. The great value of steel for toolmaking consists in a characteristic, possessed by no other substance, of becoming intensely hard when quickly cooled after it has been heated to a certain temperature. The pure, the mild steels, that nearly approach the condition of iron are ductile and weldable. On the other hand, their capacity for hardening and tempering diminishes with the comparative absence of carbon, which is the principal hardening element, though in no case does the proportion equal that in cast iron. In steel, carbon seldom amounts to more than 1·5 per cent. It is less than 1 per cent. in the mildest plates.

In addition to carbon, but in a lesser degree, manganese, phosphorus and silicon are hardening constituents of steel. Within certain limits, the more these constituents are present, the lower the temperature of the cooling liquid employed, and the greater its power of absorbing heat, the more intense will be the hardness induced in the steel. Mushet steel, used for making turning tools, is produced by the addition of woolfram or tungsten, in the form of a metallic alloy, to steel. The resulting alloy is so hard that it does not require to be hardened by the tool maker.

There is, as regards chemical composition, very little difference between wrought iron and some of the mild steels. But when working there is a very essential difference between them. Wrought iron is never perfectly homogeneous, whilst mild steel is of the same character throughout. This difference is due to the altered condition in the processes of manufacture. The fluidity of cast iron is mainly due to the presence of its carbon, and in a lesser degree to its sulphur. These are removed from the iron in the processes of puddling; and one important result is the non-fusibility of the wrought iron at the temperature at which it is found best to work it. Wrought iron is never in a state of absolute fusion at any time during the process of its puddling. It is simply brought into a pasty condition, like a lump of dough. In order to render this material more homogeneous, the pasty mass is compressed under steam hammers or tilt hammers, and is passed beneath squeezers of different types, is cut up again and re-heated, and the operations of hammering, squeezing, and rolling are repeated, the homogeneous quality of the iron improving with each repetition of these operations. These sets of operations will be repeated three or four times in the case of good merchantable iron, and it is the cost of fuel and labour involved which renders wrought iron so much more costly than cast iron.

After the last piling, re-heating, and hammering processes have been gone through, the iron is run between grooved rollers of diminishing sizes, to impart the final sectional forms to the bars or plates required for the use of the smith. But even in the best wrought iron, owing to the absence of fusion, some of the oxide or scale, and some of the impurities originally present in the iron, or taken up in the process of puddling, become mechanically mixed with, and remain in the bars, which always remain laminated, causing the iron to become spilly, and to develop incipient fracture when wrought into structures. The best wrought iron can never be depended on entirely for absolute homogeneity. But for the average work of the smith it holds its own, because of its ductility, weldability, and the general ease with which it can be fashioned into intricate forms.

The Bessemer and Siemens steels are free from this lamination, because during the process of fusion all scale or oxide is expelled; this is one reason why the mild steels have superseded wrought iron largely for boiler-makers' work, and for cranks and similar structures, where lamination would be fatal to strength and durability.

Steel being homogeneous—that is, having no lamination—is eminently adapted for forging light and delicate work, where strength, rigidity, and lightness are required in combination. While wrought iron can be worked almost at the fusing point, each different sample of steel seems to work best at a particular temperature, differing from that of other samples, but never beyond a full red heat. Steel takes a much higher polish than wrought iron, and is therefore better suited to work where good finish is necessary.

Whether steel is more troublesome to work than iron depends on the nature of the forging and on the quality of metal. For small model work, steel is by far the easier, because there is no grain to open out, besides the superior rigidity, and so forth. In large and heavy forgings there is no advantage to be gained on this score. Steel forgings of moderate size and thin sections have to be worked at a lower temperature than iron, so a larger number of heats must be taken in the former than in the latter. For the same reason the various operations should be performed more rapidly while the steel retains its heat.

There is more initial difficulty in welding steel than iron, due to the differences in various samples of steel. Once the best welding heat for any bar of steel is known, there is no more trouble experienced in welding pieces from that bar. Sand alone is used as a flux for welding iron; for steel a mixture of sand and common salt is better.

There is a greater difference of opinion as to the working of steel than there is in regard to the working of iron. The practice of allowing steel to soak in the fire, approved by some, is denounced by others. The temperature to which steel can be raised without burning it is also a matter of dispute. The practice of hardening and tempering steel opens up an unlimited field for discussion. The reasons are that steels vary in quality much more than wrought iron, and since the peculiar value of steel is due to its chemical and molecular composition, slight differences in which cause great changes in the material, and as even slight and sudden alterations in temperature are sufficient to entirely change their arrangement, it is easy to understand why, though not how, the practical working of the material is affected. Partly because of these differences and consequent differences in treatment demanded, some makes of steel are considered superior to others. Thus, a man accustomed to work in one quality mainly, and having adopted certain modes of treatment with the best results, may find the same modes do not give equally good results with another quality; he may then condemn the steel, when in reality the fault lies in wrong treatment. Every bar of new steel should be worked tentatively in order to discover the best heat and the best way to work that particular brand. Unless this is done, failure to obtain the best results will frequently follow. The practice of upsetting steel is deprecated by some. But if the steel is of good quality it will upset just as well as iron.

Steel should be made as hot as the metal will safely bear, but it must not be overheated, or it will become burnt. A higher temperature can be used on steel required for large forgings than for steel used for light work generally, and for cutting tools. Burnt steel under the hammer will crumble to pieces as though it were cast iron, and will show a coarse granulated fracture. There are, however, degrees in burning; the steel may be burnt only slightly on the surface, so slightly that it does not fracture, or, if fractured, does not show this coarsely crystalline structure ; yet its quality for cutting instruments will be sensibly impaired. The temperature at which overheating occurs varies, of course, with different qualities. If scales form and fall off, the steel is, as a rule, overheated. It is then almost impossible to restore its quality. If not burnt very badly, a good hammering on the anvil will improve it considerably.

Steel, even more than iron, should be turned around in the fire to keep the heat uniform. The blast should be slackened after the edges have become red-hot. A full cherry-red is usually considered the proper heat for forging—but this expression is rather vague, and the temperature will vary with different qualities. Hammering should not be continued after the steel has lost its redness.

There is a temperature in steel corresponding with what is termed in iron a "black heat"—at which it is not safe to work it. Experiments show that a steel plate heated, and allowed to cool, suffers no diminution of strength, but that while cooling, and while at a blue heat, any hammering or bending seriously injures the metal. The blue heat corresponds with any temperature between about 470° and 600°.

Steel used for making tools is classified according to the percentage of carbon it contains, to which the following list is a guide. *Razor temper steel* (1½ per cent. carbon) is so easily spoilt by being overheated that it can be worked only in the hands of a very skilful workman. When properly heated, it will do twice the work of ordinary tool steel for turning chilled rolls, etc. *Saw-file temper steel* (1⅜ per cent. carbon) requires careful treatment, and although it will stand more heat than razor steel, should not be heated above a cherry red. *Tool temper* steel (1¼ per cent. carbon) is the most useful for turning tools, drills, and planing-machine tools, and it may be forged by ordinary workmen. It is possible, with great care and skill, to weld cast steel of this temper. *Spindle temper* steel (1⅛ per cent. carbon) is very useful for circular cutters, large turning tools, taps, screwing dies etc. This temper requires considerable care in welding. *Chisel temper* steel (1 per cent. carbon) combines great toughness in the unhardened state, with the capacity of hardening at a low heat. It is consequently well adapted for tools when the unhardened part is required to stand the blow of a hammer without splitting, but where a hard cutting edge is required, such as cold chisels, hot setts, etc. *Sett temper* steel ($\frac{7}{8}$ per cent. carbon) is adapted for tools, such as cold setts, the unhardened parts of which have to stand very heavy blows. *Die temper* steel ($\frac{3}{4}$ per cent. carbon) is the most suitable for tools of which the surface only is required to be hard, and where the capacity to withstand great pressure is of importance, such as stamping or pressing dies, boiler cups, etc. The last two tempers may be easily welded by a mechanic accustomed to work cast steel.

The process of hardening, as commonly understood by smiths, means the heating of a piece of steel to redness and quickly plunging it into a cooling liquid, usually either water or oil. Hardening steel often causes it to crack and warp. On immersing the steel into the cooling medium, the outer covering is rapidly cooled off first, and shrinks upon the interior. The shrinkage puts the outside in tension. Presently the interior cools, but it is prevented from free shrinkage by its union with the exterior, and is thus itself put in tension. Then one of two things may happen : either there will be a condition of permanent tension, productive of warping or curvature, or the stresses will find relief in fracture.

Steel that is heated to redness and allowed to cool slowly is said to be annealed. Steel may be annealed by making it red hot and allowing it to cool between hot cinders. Or it may be left in a low fire until the fire has gone out and the cinders have become cold. Or it may be enclosed in a box with charcoal powder, raised to a red heat, and allowed to become cold. By hardening, steel is made intensely hard, by tempering it is made softer and less brittle, but yet it remains very hard ; by annealing, it is brought into its softest possible condition.

The principal hardening agent is cold water; salt water, lukewarm water, and oil are sometimes used. Mercury is also very efficient, but its expense precludes its use for ordinary work, and for most purposes pure cold water only is used. For light and delicate work oil is generally considered preferable, and it is customary to use oil or tallow in preference to water for all delicate work. In order to lessen the liability to curvature, long narrow articles are immersed perpendicularly instead of horizontally or diagonally in the fluid, so that its effect may be evenly distributed over the whole of the surface. Steel is apt to crack if it is taken out of the water before being thoroughly quenched, or if the water level is kept at one place ; it should therefore be moved slightly up and down in the water. When dipping an article of unequal thickness on the edges, the thicker edge, as a rule, should be dipped first, to lessen risk of cracking. Smiths have an opinion that water which has been long used is preferable to fresh water, so they do not change the water in their hardening tanks, but simply add sufficient fresh to make up for waste. This preference may be due to the fact that warming of the water by immersing red-hot metal drives off the air contained in it, and allows the fluid to come into more intimate contact with the surface of the steel. The belief that boiling the water for hardening steel is an improvement may be explained in the same way.

It is not necessary that hardening should always be done in a liquid. A thin heated plate placed between two pieces of cold metal will become hardened as effectually as if immersed in water or oil. This is often done, because it tends to lessen risk of warping in a plate.

Hardening by means of hammer blows is of occasional service to increase the elasticity and hardness of a plate or lamina of steel. Its effect is similar to that of cold rolling and wire drawing, and is removed by annealing. If hammer hardening is prolonged too far the metal is fractured ; annealing must therefore be resorted to before this stage is reached. The range of temper obtainable in hammer hardening is not great, and it has a limited value, being confined chiefly to laminated springs.

Tempering means that the hardened steel is slightly re-heated, and when at a certain known temperature, indicated by a shade of colour which appears on its brightened surface, it is plunged into a cooling liquid, or in some few cases is allowed to cool gradually in air. This heat for tempering differs in almost every variety of tool or piece of mechanism. The tints through which steel passes from the lower to the higher temperature are straw, gold or yellow, chocolate, purple, violet, and blue. The greatest hardness and elasticity combined is obtained by tempering at a straw colour. Hardening by quenching at a red heat makes a tool intensely hard, but brittle. Tempering by quenching at a blue makes it elastic, but soft. Between these extremes lies the whole practice of hardening and tempering.

All cutting tools of the same type are not tempered alike. Thus, a tool for working hard cast steel will be tempered harder than one for working grey cast iron. A tool tempered a straw colour is harder than one tempered a blue; so that if tools for hard steel are tempered to a straw, those for soft iron and brass are tempered at a tint approaching purple.

As an example of hardening and tempering, a cold chisel is the tool selected. The scale is removed from the surface, and its cutting end, to the length of about a couple of inches, is then first heated to a cherry red in a clear fire, afterwards quenching in water, and thus hardened. It is taken out and rapidly brightened with a bit of grindstone or emery, in order that the rapidly changing hues may be observed the better. The cooling of the end only lasts for an instant, as the heat of the shank at once raises the temperature of the end for tempering, until the instant arrives at which it must be quenched. The smith then plunges the entire chisel into the water, moving it to and fro until quite cold. The colour for tempering in the case of a cold chisel is a deep straw inclining to purple, but, of course, the colour will vary with different grades of steel.

Another way of tempering small tools is to heat to redness in the forge fire a bar of iron, and lay the tools upon it until they reach the colour required, and to then quench them. If the bar is made red hot at one end only, the tools can be gradually slid along toward that end and so slowly heated thoroughly through, until they reach the precise tint desired for tempering.

A bath of molten lead is a good heating agent for articles that are of unequal thickness; these can thus be heated uniformly. The lead is prevented from oxidation by covering its surface with powdered charcoal. The temperature of a bath of molten metal is of course uniform, and by making alloys of lead and tin in various proportions, an extensive range of temperature is obtainable. The table on p. 153 serves to show what range can be got by such tempering baths.

Drills for cutting iron are tempered to a dark straw at the cutting edges. The remarks made in reference to the hardening and tempering of a cold chisel apply equally to drills for iron. Drills for hard steel are heated and quenched in a lump of lead, and not tempered afterwards.

Axes are hardened and tempered very much like chisels. They are heated first to redness, and quenched in water to a depth of two or three inches. A face is polished, and the changing tints observed until the appearance of a deep blue, when total immersion is made for temper. As for other tools, different shades of blue, inclining towards a brown straw, will be required for different grades of steel.

TEMPERING STEEL.

Colour.	Articles to be Tempered.	Composition of the Bath.		Tempera-ture in de-grees Fah.
		Lead.	Tin.	
Yellowish tint	Lancets	7	4	420°
	Other surgical instru-ments	7½	4	430°
	Razors, etc.	8	4	442°
Pale yellow ...	Penknives, and some implements of sur-gery	8½	4	450°
Straw yellow	Larger penknives, scalpels, etc. ...	10	4	470°
	Scissors, shears, gar-den hoes, cold chisels, etc. ...	14	4	490°
Brown yellow	Axes, firmer chisels, plane irons, pocket-knives, etc. ...	19	4	509-
Light purple	Table-knives, large shears, etc. ...	30	4	530°
Dark purple	Swords, watch-springs, etc.	48	4	550°
Clear blue ...	Largesprings, daggers, augers, fine saws, etc.	50	2	558°
Pale blue ...	Pit saws, hand saws, and some springs	Boiling linseed oil.		600°
Greenish blue	Articles which require to be somewhat softer	Molten lead.		612°

Mill picks are hardened only, and not tempered. They are heated to a dark red, and quenched, the temper thus obtained not let down, as is the case with most of the tools already noticed. Pure soft water is quite suitable for these, though some smiths use mixtures of salt, alum, sal-ammoniac, etc.

Springs are hardened in the usual way by heating to a cherry red, and quenching in water. Then they are smeared with tallow or lard, and heated over the fire, moving them to and fro until the tallow catches fire, and blazes and burns off. The springs are then laid upon the forge, or in the ashes to cool down. If the work is of irregular thickness, the burning of the oil should be repeated two or three times. Small springs made in quantities are often put into a sheet-iron pan and covered with oil, and held over the fire until the oil blazes and burns off. Moving and shaking the pan about causes the temper to be more uniform. In the case of heavy springs the operation may be repeated two or three times.

Screw taps are conveniently heated in an iron tube, large enough to allow not only of the admission of the tap, but also of the tongs by which it is held. The tap is first heated gradually and very slowly, and equally throughout, to a dull red in the tube. If heated rapidly, the edges of the threads will be made hotter than the interior, and being too hard, will probably crumble off in use. It must be an invariable rule to harden and temper taps at the lowest heat practicable. A dull red must not be exceeded. It is better to make two or three attempts, increasing the heat each time, rather than to overheat the tap, which is plunged vertically into water and held there until quite cold. Afterwards the flutes are brightened and the tap heated in the tube to a light straw. Some use linseed oil baths for hardening taps and dies. The points of the threads will be protected if coated with soft soap, or with a paste made of prussiate of potash and flour, or yeast.

Screwing dies are heated to a cherry red, and hardened in salt water. To diminish the risk of cracking, they may be covered with prussiate of potash or with a paste of soap and oil. The faces are polished, and to temper them the dies placed on a piece of hot iron, taking care to turn them over and over until they are of a straw colour. A bath of linseed oil may be used for cooling. Worn dies are, as a rule, re-cut, but before this can be done, the temper must be completely drawn by annealing the dies by heating them to a light cherry red in a clear fire and allowing them to cool slowly. Other tools, such as broaches, milling cutters, reamers, and lip drills, when worn, are similarly annealed preparatory to re-cutting. Afterwards they are hardened and tempered just as in the case of new tools.

Case hardening is a method commonly used for rendering the surface of wrought-iron as hard as tempered steel. Case hardening means that just the outer skin of iron is hardened, and made of the nature of steel. Only wrought iron can be treated thus. A mere film of surface hardening may be effected by heating the iron red-hot, rolling it in powdered yellow prussiate of potash, and quenching in water. When the hardening is required to extend to a greater depth, the work is enclosed in an iron receptacle along with leather clippings, bones, horn, and yellow prussiate of potash, and heated for from twenty to forty hours. The work is then cooled in water. The advantages of case hardening are that the toughness of the wrought iron is combined with a durable wearing surface as hard as steel; and that the first cost of the forgings, and of the cost of their being tooled and finished into shape, is less than the cost of steel forgings. Case hardening is adopted in link-reversing gear for engines, for the eyes and working faces of levers, for pins or pivots, and so forth. To case harden at the forge, have ready a quantity of yellow prussiate of potash powdered very fine in an iron tray. Heat the work in the clear fire to red heat and with a spoon strew thickly over the surface of the forging, and, if practicable, roll the forging also in the potash. The work is re-heated and time given to allow the powder to fuse and run freely over the surface, then the forging is quenched, and this hardens it.

INDEX.